To my daughter -my steady place in this world. You have carried my heart through storms you never saw, and you have given me more reasons to keep going than you will ever understand.

INTRODUCTION

I am not a professional writer.

There will be typos in this book, and the grammar police will probably have a lot to say.

I am simply a woman who sat down one day and began typing her story.

This book was written by an ordinary, everyday person, without a publisher or a professional editor.

I am not trying to become rich or famous. I don't care if I never make it into Oprah's Book Club.

I wrote this for one reason only, to let others know they are not alone, not in their fear, not in their experiences, and not in their shame.

Disclaimer

This book is a work of memoir based on the author's personal experiences and recollections. Certain names, identifying details, locations, timelines, and characteristics have been changed or omitted to protect the privacy of individuals and to preserve anonymity.

MY LAST LETTER TO ALABAMA

CHAPTER ONE: WHERE MY STORY BEGINS

I never thought I'd write a book. Then again, I never thought my life would be the kind of story people might actually want to read. It's been one long stretch of storms, one after another.

These days, the skies are calmer, but for the first forty years or so, Lord, what a ride that was. So here I am, finally putting it all down on paper. My hope, my goal, is that, maybe my story will help someone else weather their own storm a little easier.

I am not writing this book to hurt, belittle, expose or destroy. I am writing to release all the things I hid from the world; from myself. I thought I had to keep all this pain inside so the world wouldn't know how much ugliness I have experienced. How damaged I was, and at sometimes still am. But through experience, time, education and strength- I've come to the realization, that I can let go of everything that has ever hurt and set it free from my mind.

When I was born, to say I was a surprise would be putting it gently. Still, I came along, the caboose of a tired train that had already seen plenty of miles. We didn't have much, but as kids, we didn't feel poor. There was food on the table, clothes on our backs, and laughter in the house.

My memories, full of sounds like the screen door slamming, kids playing in the yard, and the smell of Mama in the kitchen, frying up potatoes and onions. When I think back on my childhood, the instant memories are happy ones.

We lived in a big, two-story house that was beautiful but nearly impossible to keep warm in the winter. When the cold set in, we'd pile into the same bed, stacking quilts on top of each other, just trying to stay warm.

I don't really remember ever sleeping alone. I was always curled up in someone's bed, wherever someone had the patience for me that night.

But today, nighttime is when the memories flood in, filling my mind when everything else goes quiet.

It is where my earliest pieces come back to me, the first memories of trauma I experienced as a child.

I can vividly remember being in their bedroom, in their bed, sitting on top of them, and the truth is, I wasn't scared or confused. I was comfortable. Safe, even. They were someone I trusted completely, someone who, at times, tucked me in at night and made me laugh.

What happened didn't feel wrong. It felt as normal as if they were rubbing my back or brushing my hair. It was show and tell. Show me yours and I'll show you mine.

That's the part that's hardest to explain to anyone who hasn't lived it. It didn't feel like a violation.

It felt like we were playing a game. It felt like attention. And as a little girl, at the tender age I was, I didn't know the difference between the right and the wrong kind of attention; especially from someone I felt safe with.

I won't go into details about the abuse. It's too personal. But I can tell you that being taught those kind of things at such a young age changes how you see yourself and how you understand love.

As little girls, we are taught to play with babies, and play house. Wash clothes, cook dinner and be a wife and mother.

Coupled with how we are programmed from infancy, trauma can quietly shape what we believe love looks like. I learned early on that sex was how a man showed interest in me, that it meant approval, that it meant I was wanted.

Those beliefs didn't announce themselves loudly. They settled in quietly and became part of how I moved through the world. I didn't see myself as someone with boundaries that needed protecting, only as someone who needed to be liked, accepted, wanted. Attention felt like validation, and validation felt like safety.

I didn't yet understand that the way I had learned love made me vulnerable, that it taught me to ignore my own discomfort and trust the wrong people. I carried that confusion with me into adolescence, not knowing how easily it could be taken advantage of.

When I was fourteen, I had an experience that would shape how I saw myself for years. I was spending time with a couple of boys I thought were friends. They were the ones who introduced me to drinking.

I didn't want to say no, even though it tasted awful. I took small sips anyway, trying to fit in, trying to seem older, trying to be liked.

At first, I remember laughing and feeling relaxed, like I belonged. Then the tiredness hit, heavy and sudden, stronger than it should have been. I had not drank that much, why was I so intoxicated? My body felt disconnected from my mind. The boys were across the room, distracted with games, so I lay down on the bed, telling myself I just needed to rest.

When I woke up, something was wrong. My head felt thick and foggy, my body slow and unresponsive. I couldn't piece together how I had gotten there or how much time had passed. I remember waking briefly, then slipping away again, each time seeing a different boys face.

The memories come in fragments, broken and incomplete, but the feeling was clear. I had not chosen what was being done to my body by the two boys. I couldn't move. I couldn't speak. I felt frozen in my own body.

I was too intoxicated to fight back, and when I attempted to get up, I was told to lay my ass back down. I was so embarrassed. How could they do this to such a young girl. Had they been monsters this whole time? Hiding in plain sight? How could I not see this in them?

When it was over, I carried the secret like a weight no one could see. I went quiet, holding it close, afraid of what would happen if I ever let it out. I didn't know what to do with that amount of humiliation. Was I supposed to hate them? Report them? Or was I to blame for putting myself in that position?

At fourteen, how was I supposed to process that kind of trauma? In my mind, I was now a whore, and nobody could ever find out. I told myself to forget, to move on, to pretend it hadn't happened. I knew if I told anyone, they'd say it was my fault, that I shouldn't have been there, shouldn't have been drinking. So, I stayed silent.

Not long after, my father took a new position with his company. We moved several states away to beautiful Alabama. I had never see so many tall beautiful green trees. They felt inviting, fresh and new, like they had been waiting for me, offering protection from what I had left behind.

I saw that move as my escape. Moving so far from the place I had lived my whole life felt like a clean slate, where no one knew what I had been through. I left that girl behind, or at least I tried to.

When I started my new school, I tried to blend in and be a normal teenager again. I had a couple of boyfriends, but at fifteen, most boys only wanted one thing.

I was still searching for something real, something that felt like love, but we didn't stay in that town long enough for anything to last. After about a year, we moved again, same state, different town.

Every move felt like starting over, and somewhere along the way, I got tired of pretending to be fine. I didn't want to make new friends and stayed in touch with the ones from the last town.

I remember having lunch with a close friend at a local burger shop. She introduced me to a guy, a friend of a friend. He was a grown man, far too old for a fifteen-year-old girl. He was six years older than me.

But I thought he was so handsome. And he was very sweet to me. I didn't know it then, but I now I understand, he saw exactly how naive I was and used it to his advantage .

He bought me gifts, told me I was beautiful, said all the right things a lonely, chubby, fifteen-year-old girl wants to hear, and I believed him. Every single word.

I was still a child. But at the time, I thought I had found a man who thought would take care of me. Who thought I mattered. Who loved and would protect me.

Looking back, I can't understand how anyone thought it was

okay, how my parents allowed it. Why were they allowing this grown man date their little girl? Were they tired of raising kids? Did they want me gone? Those are hard questions to ask, but they're the truth that still lingers. Nobody stopped him. Nobody stepped in.

And while I thought he was a knight in shinning armour, the truth is, he was thief, stealing what was left of my childhood.

I'd been trained to play house all my life, so it made sense that at just sixteen, I quit school and left home to get married. At the time, I thought I was grown, thought I was in control.

But now, I know I was just a child trying to survive something I didn't have words for yet. I wasn't chasing love; I was chasing a fantasy. I was trying to turn something broken into something that looked normal.

That is where my story begins. And even though it starts in a dark place, it is not where it ends. Somehow, through all of it, I kept finding pieces of light, enough to guide me forward even when I could not see the way.

CHAPTER TWO: THE ILLUSION OF LOVE

Marriage wasn't what I thought it would be. I had dreamed of security, of building a life with someone who would protect and love me. But what I got was something else entirely.

All those gifts he used to buy me, the dinners, the small tokens that made me feel special, they were paid for with bill money that never got paid. We had nothing. No TV, no books, no radio, and no food half the time. Just four walls and a silence that felt heavier by the day.

There were days I didn't eat until he came home, and when he did, he'd bring me a cheeseburger and fries like it was some kind of treat. That was our dinner most nights, greasy food, cigarettes, and regret. I was barely sixteen, trying to play the role of a wife to a man who was barely functioning himself. He didn't know how to manage money, and I didn't either. We lived day to day, paycheck to paycheck, pretending it was normal. It wasn't love. It was survival.

I remember the day my daddy brought over a kitchen table they no longer needed. We didn't have one, so he loaded it up and came to drop it off. My husband was at work.

Daddy carried the table inside and started putting the chairs together while I sat on the floor, watching him. Every turn of the screwdriver made my heart ache a little more. I wanted to tell him everything, that I thought I was pregnant, I was scared, and wanted to go home.

With each chair he assembled, I searched for a way to ask him to take me home. But the words never came. My pride, my shame and my secrets held my mouth shut.

When he finished, he stood up, dusted his hands, looked at me and smiled before walking out the door. I watched from the window as he drove away. I watched his truck drive down the road and I cried until my chest hurt.

In that moment, it felt like I had wandered into a forest so deep that no one could see me or hear me anymore. I felt erased. The carefree life of a teenager slipped away, and what remained felt heavy and unfamiliar.

That moment has stayed with me all my life, the day I realized I had built myself a cage and did not know how to get out.

Next came the anger. My husband's resentment toward me grew with each passing day, like he suddenly realized he had made a mistake too. He couldn't take care of himself, much less a wife, and now there was a baby on the way. He tried to act happy about it, but the truth showed in his eyes.

What neither of us had considered was my health. With every month that passed, I got sicker. The morning sickness never stopped; it was all day, every day. I could barely stand long enough to make him dinner without running to the bathroom, throwing up until my ribs hurt.

He thought I was doing it on purpose, just trying to get out of cooking. The funny part was, we didn't even have a stove, just an old electric skillet that I used to heat up canned food. That was our life: cheap meals, resentment and long days that all looked the same.

I spent most of my time alone, sick, scared, and unsure what was happening to my body. I quit smoking because it made me violently nauseous, and I knew it wasn't good for the baby.

But nothing else seemed to help. I had no appetite, no energy, and no doctor to tell me if the baby was okay. I didn't have insurance, and since I got pregnant before we were married, his job's insurance wouldn't cover it either.

Some days I couldn't get off the couch. I felt weak, dizzy, and completely drained. But he didn't see that. He started calling me names, lazy ass, like being sick was something I'd chosen.

He'd say, "You're just pregnant, not dying," and I believed him. I had never been pregnant before. I didn't know what was normal or what wasn't. I had no phone to call my mama and no one to turn to for help.

So, I just lay there, day after day, believing maybe he was right, maybe I really am just a lazy ass.

With the sickness and the unhealthy living came the nightmares. I didn't know it at the time, but looking back, I'm sure it was tied to high blood pressure from the pregnancy.

One night, I had a dream so vivid and horrifying that I can

still feel it to this day. I dreamed my husband came home from work, took me upstairs to the baby's room, hung my pregnant body on a meat hook, and let his hunting dogs eat me.

I woke up in a cold sweat, terrified and shaking. I woke him up, but even as I did, I was sick with fear of him. Deep down, it felt like more than just a nightmare, it felt like a warning.

If I knew then what I know now, I would have left that very day. Because that dream was an omen. It was God's way of telling me to run, to flee from him as fast as I could.

But I was sixteen, pregnant, scared, and too ashamed to call my parents. I felt trapped, convinced I had no choice but to stay.

This is when the hitting started. He never punched me square in the face, but he'd slap me upside the head, shove me onto the sofa, hold me down with his full weight just to prove he was in control. He wanted everything his way. If he wanted to watch an old war movie, that's what we watched.

If he wanted to read in silence, I had to be quiet and leave him alone. My opinions didn't matter. My wants didn't exist. I was a piece of furniture, there for his comfort when he needed or wanted me.

If a friend stopped by and asked me to go somewhere, he'd get angry, even if he had no plans to talk to me or spend time with me himself.

He wanted me there, silent, obedient, present. And if I ever went anyway, I'd pay for it later. The fights that followed weren't always loud, but they were cruel. When I asked him to stop hitting me, he'd smirk and say he wasn't "hitting" me, that I was being dramatic.

Somehow, he always found a way to make me question my own reality.

One night, while we were watching one of his old war movies, I felt something strange in my stomach. It wasn't pain at first, just a heavy, unsettling feeling that didn't seem right. I stood up, and in that instant, blood ran down both of my legs. I froze, terrified. I was about three and a half months pregnant. I ran to the bathroom, shaking, and when I sat down, large clots of blood were coming out of me. Panic took over. I told him we had to go to the hospital, but he got angry, saying I was overreacting.

Still, I begged him until he finally gave in, but mentioned we didn't really have the money to waste driving to the hospital.

We made the hour-long trip to the hospital in silence. I sat in the passenger seat with towels under me, trying to keep the blood from soaking through. That's how bad it was. Every mile felt like a lifetime.

Once we got to the hospital, it was incredibly packed and the wait time was going to be a long time. He was so irritated with having to sit in the waiting room, and then finally they took me back, got me in a gown, and got me in a room.

He went outside to smoke, and it seemed like he was out there the entire time. A doctor came in and checked me. He said that my cervix looked good, that sometimes there's bleeding in pregnancies.

They took my blood pressure and it was a little high. They were going to keep me for a little while to see if my blood pressure went down and to check if I had any contractions. They hooked me up to some machines, and we were there for hours on end, but they said that everything looked good, and so they let me go home.

Of course, my husband mentioned that he was right, there wasn't anything wrong with me and we could have saved that gas money.

The ride home was quiet because we were both tired, but he did manage to ask me if I would give him a blowjob while he was driving the car.

As you can imagine, I felt so unseen, unloved, and minimal. I don't know how else to explain it.

The fact that I had gone through this, felt like I was going to lose the pregnancy, scared out of my mind due to all the blood I had lost, but he still managed to ask for that.

As time went on, we were not able to pay our bills. We were still living paycheck to paycheck, and eventually, we couldn't pay our rent and had to go live with one of his aunts.

They barely had any extra room, but they did have one small bedroom that had a twin bed in it, and that's where we lived for about a month. And of course, the bed was too small for the both of us and he said he should get the bed because he is the one who had to get up and go to work.

Then we moved into a house that I'm pretty sure should have been condemned. It looked like it had been vacant for a decade or so. It was on well water, which I probably shouldn't have been drinking during my pregnancy.

It did have a stove, but it didn't have a refrigerator. We didn't have our own bed, just had a small mattress, which we put on the floor in the living room. In all honesty, we looked like homeless people who moved into an abandoned house. That's what it felt like too.

This house was about twenty miles from where my husband worked, way out in the country. There were no neighbors, no phone, and due to it being extremely cold and the well freezing up, I then had no running water.

We had no source of heat other than the stove, and to say that this was the worst possible scenario for anybody to live in is an understatement, especially somebody who had a troubled pregnancy.

Again, I had no way of keeping food because I had no refrigerator. I had peanut butter and jelly, and that's what I ate during the day.

As a pregnant woman, I would eat a peanut butter and jelly sandwich during the day, and then my husband would come home and bring a pizza and a two-liter of Dr Pepper. Those were my meals during my pregnancy.

I remember it being Christmas while we lived there, the first one in my life I wasn't with my family. They had driven back to Texas for Christmas and I was too ashamed to tell them I didn't have money to buy presents or go anywhere, so I stayed behind.

It was the worst Christmas of my life. I had never known depression like that before. I kept asking myself, how did I end up here? Who lives like this?

I remember writing my mother a letter, begging her to come and get me. I told her everything. I confessed all the ugliness and hate I was enduring, the conditions I was living in.

I walked down the long driveway in the cold wind, to the mailbox. I put the letter inside and laid enough change for a stamp on top, with a handwritten note to the postal carrier explaining that I had no way to get to the post office to buy a stamp.

I raised the flag on the mailbox and walked back to the house. Then I waited.

A couple of weeks went by.

I finally walked back down the driveway, hoping, praying, that maybe my mother had written me back. I opened the mailbox, anxious, desperate.

My letter was still there.
The money was still there.
The note was still there.

Nothing had been touched.

I instantly began crying. I took the letter out, tore it into pieces, took it home and burned it.

Here I was, over half way into my pregnancy, no prenatal care, miserable, alone, and hopeless. Shortly after, my birthday came and went like it was just another day. But hey, I did get pizza and Dr. Pepper for dinner.

Eventually, tax season rolled around. We got our income tax return and were able to afford to get an apartment back in town, and so we moved.

For a little while, things seemed okay. I finally got in to see a doctor, and he said everything looked good, my blood pressure was fine, and the baby seemed healthy.

It was the beginning of spring. I was starting to gather things for the baby's room. My sister has mailed me a cute baby outfit with some little socks. I was starting to really get excited about being a mommy.

My parents were planning a trip back home soon, and asked if I wanted to go. The doctor said it should be fine as long as we stopped and I walked around every few hours.

It was the night before the trip, and I wanted to spend time with husband since I wasn't going to see him for a whole week.

But of course, in the evenings, this was "his time" and spending time with me was never on his agenda.

He got angry, said all I ever did was nag and complain, and want attention.

I started crying, and he sat down in front of me, grabbed my head, and slammed his forehead into my face. The impact broke one of my bottom teeth.

The pain was intense. I ran to the bathroom crying, and he followed, apologizing over and over, mostly because he knew my parents would see it the next day.

I told my mother the next morning that I had hit my mouth on the bathtub while getting out. I can still remember the look in her eyes; I think deep down she knew that wasn't true. But she never asked.

The trip back to Texas went fine at first. We made it to my sister's house, and I felt relieved just to be somewhere safe. I slept well that first night, and the next morning we were sitting around the kitchen table having breakfast when I felt a dull cramp in my stomach.

I thought I just needed to use the bathroom. But when I went, there was a small amount of blood on the tissue paper. I told my mom, and we tried to stay calm. A few minutes later, the cramps started again.

I was too young to understand what was happening, but my mom began timing them. That's when she realized, they were contractions.

She drove me to the hospital, and the doctors confirmed it. I was in labor. I was only six and a half months along. They did everything they could to stop it, but they couldn't.

My son was born weighing just a pound and a half.

He lived for only six hours before he passed away. One minute I was a teenage girl, the next, the mother of a dead infant son. Very surreal.

While we were at the funeral, my dad came up and hugged me. For a moment, I felt that old familiar pull, the part of me that just wanted him to take me home.

I kept thinking, if I just told him the truth, how my husband treated me, the things he had done, would he scoop me up and rescue me from this nightmare? Or would he tell me that I am a big girl now and must deal with it on my own.

But I kept quiet, said nothing. I had made this mess, and I had to live with it and stay hidden in this web of lies I had been keeping from my family.

After the death of my child I buried the pain deep inside. My husband would not let me grieve.

He kept saying there was nothing we could do, that I needed to stop crying and get over it.

He refused to talk about it and acted like it never happened. That kind of trauma eats away at you. I spent my days sleeping, eating, and staying up all night watching TV.

At seventeen years old, I was living like a hermit. My friends stopped coming over and I could not go anywhere or do anything without risking another fight.

One night, I convinced him to go out with my best friend and her boyfriend. We actually had fun. Got a little too drunk!

I thought I just had a bad hangover the next morning, but the days passed, and I realized it was not a hangover. I was pregnant again, only four months after losing my son.

I dreaded telling my mom because I knew she would be furious. When I finally did, she told me that she and Dad were moving back to Texas.

I was devastated. I had never lived that far from my parents before. Even though I had been living on my own for about a year, it still felt as though they wer leaving me behind.

I desperately wanted to go with them. I remember being there when they moved away. Again, I watched my dad drive that truck down the road. I wanted to run after them. Scream and beg them to take me with them. But again, I remained quiet.

That fall, things between me and my husband were surprisingly good. Out of the ten years we were together, that short stretch was the only time we had anything close to a loving relationship.

I think he was afraid of losing another baby, so he was gentle and kind. We moved out to the country into a small two-bedroom house. It wasn't much, but for the first time in a long time, it felt like a home.

This is when I became close with his mother. She seemed like a free spirit. I had never known a mother like her. She dressed young for her age, wore lots of make-up, curled her hair, and was flirtatious.

She was really totally opposite of my mom. Not in a bad way. I loved my mother, but my mother was the typical mom.

And my mother did not care about being fancy, painted up, or draw attention to herself at all. His mother did. She liked attention.

She was really just learning how to live herself. She became a mother at a young age and had children to tend to. Her husband died when the children were young and then she attached herself to the first man she found, which was an unemployed alcoholic, that her children despised.

At this time in her life, she was just living her best life, she just couldn't afford it financially. So, she moved in with us.

I didn't mind at all, because we were more like friends than mother and daughter in law. But my husband, at this point and time, did not approve of how his mother was living.

She was loving her life, dating and just enjoying being single and free. I remember one time; she had went out on a date. They came back and he was dropping her off.

They were kissing in the car out in the front yard and my husband had a fit and asked her to move out if she was going to act like a whore.

She left the next week. But she and I kept in touch and would have lunch and go shopping together.

As my pregnancy went on, I gained a lot of weight, developed gestational diabetes, and my blood pressure stayed high. At one appointment, my doctor checked my pressure and immediately admitted me to the hospital. I was on the verge of a stroke.

They did an emergency C-section, and my second child was born healthy and beautiful.

My parents came out, and Mom stayed a couple of weeks before Dad came back to take her home. I cried watching her leave. How was I supposed to take care of this tiny baby all by myself?

Months went by and things stayed okay until my husband started drinking. Maybe the pressure of having a wife and baby finally got to him.

One morning he went fishing with his friends and did not come home. By two in the morning, I was worried sick.

When I called, I found out he was drunk at his friend's house, sitting by a fire with friends, some of them women I did not know.

I loaded my newborn in the car and drove twenty something miles to get him. He was so drunk we had to stop several times so he could vomit.

I was furious. If I had done something like that, he would have beaten me half to death. But for him, it was always different.

When our baby was about five months old, I started working part-time as a waitress. It gave us extra money and gave me something I had not had in a long time, a bit of freedom. I loved it, he hated it.

Then one day, out of nowhere, he said he wanted to move to Texas, I was beyond happy, I was thrilled to be going home.

I thought this move would be a new beginning for us. But I had no idea it would open the door to a whole new kind of hell for me.

CHAPTER THREE: BEHIND CLOSED DOORS

Moving home was supposed to be a fresh start. We sold everything we could not fit into our small car, the one my parents had given me. The air conditioner did not work, but otherwise, it was a good car.

We loaded up one hot June morning and headed on our way. The trip was long and miserable, but we finally arrived in Texas with a tired five-month-old baby and barely any money to our name.

We stayed with my parents for the first few months, and the sense of safety I felt there was indescribable. I had not felt that secure in such a long time. But I knew it could not last forever. Our money was running out. My husband could not find work, but truthfully, he was not trying very hard either.

I would write letters back in Alabama to my best friend and to my mother-in-law to let her know how we were doing and to send her pictures of our son. She would always write back and I enjoyed sending and receiving those letters.

I always thought it funny that I got along with his mother, and he got along with mine. He and my mother got along amazingly well.

They would sit for hours drinking coffee, smoking cigarettes, and talking. I was jealous because I had never experienced that kind of closeness with him. I believe his mother was jealous of the relationship they had too.

Deep down, I knew he had no real interest in me beyond sex and having a wife to cook and clean for him. He never cared about what I liked, what I thought, or what I wanted to become. Not once.

He never even asked what I wanted from life. It was obvious to see that, in his eyes, I was done with my achievements. Wife, mother. Done.

In August, my husband went to stay with my brother, who ran a construction crew in Fort Worth. He have my husband a job.

I stayed at mom's house with my baby boy. I was happy to stay and relieved, actually. Even that early in our marriage, I already knew I despised him and felt relief every time I was away from him.

After a while, I knew I would have to go stay with him again, and I did. We lived at my brother's house for about four months before the renters in my old childhood home moved out.

My parents still owned the house, and Mom said we could

live there rent-free until my husband found steady work. So, we moved back to my hometown, into the house where I grew up.

It felt good to have our own place again, but it was hard. We were broke and barely getting by. My husband found a job at a warehouse, but it barely paid enough to cover the gas to get there and back.

We had a toddler in diapers, and he spent what little money we had on cigarettes, dipping tobacco, and even cowboy magazines that cost five dollars a piece. That may not sound like much, but when you are counting every dollar for groceries, diapers, and the light bill, it adds up.

That is when the real fighting started. The real hitting. The choking. The kind of violent, ugly abuse that changes who you are inside.

This was when I began to see how truly evil he was, not just on the outside, but deep in his soul. He was simply a mean man. I had once believed he would be a good father, but I was wrong.

He barely provided for us. He never went anywhere with us, never went outside to play, never wanted to go to the park. As long as we were inside and sitting beside him, he would halfway interact with our son, but that was the extent of it.

He was not a man who participated in our life. It was always his rules, his way, or not at all.

Things got hard for us. We were barely making any money, our car broke down, and he lost his job. We were desperate. Then my son got sick.

He started throwing up one Thursday evening, and it continued through the weekend. By Monday night, I was terrified. I ran across the street and called a friend to take me to the emergency room. My eleven-month-old baby had seizures the entire way to the hospital.

When we got to the ER, they transported him by ambulance to a larger hospital an hour away. I rode in the car behind the ambulance, praying the whole way.

When we arrived, I waited for the doctor, a neurologist, to come speak with me. He knelt on the floor beside me and gently said that my son would not make it through the night. He had bacterial meningitis, and it was severe.

The doctor said that if he did survive, he would likely have major neurological deficits. I was dumbstruck. I had no idea what I was facing. I was in shock, flat-broke, and had no insurance. I didn't know what was about to happen. My husband was absolutely no support at all.

My parents showed up. My father took my husband back to our house, bought the parts for our car, and got it running again.

The hospital had a hotel inside it, and we qualified for financial assistance, so they donated us a room. The next twenty-four hours were critical.

Our local pastor came to the hospital and prayed over our child.

Two days later, he was still alive. The neurologist told us we would have to wait and see how his brain function recovered. Another two days passed, and they said it was a miracle. My son was healthy, and his brain function was fully intact.

I, however, was not. I was completely drained, physically, mentally, and emotionally. My husband and I had fought the entire time because he had been so distant.

He got angry when I cried and all he wanted to do was stay in the hotel room watching TV while our baby fought for his life.

The hospital allowed us to eat for free in the cafeteria, and all he did was lie in bed and be useless.

I remember writing a letter to Alabama to his mother to let her know what was going on, she had gotten a few phone calls, but I wanted to update her in my own way.

I started getting sick and thought it was from stress, but no, as fate would have it, I was pregnant again. No jobs, broken down car, baby sick in the hospital; and I was pregnant. What a month.

After two weeks, we took our son home. It was Christmas. I only had one toy for him, a crib mobile that looked like a little television and played an underwater scene with fish. He loved it.

He was still just an infant, too young to understand what Christmas was, but it broke my heart that I couldn't buy him anything else. There is no worse feeling than not being able to give your child gifts at Christmas.

Once again, I had to tell my mother that I was pregnant. And once again, she was furious with me.

My husband had finally found a job, but of course, since I was already pregnant, his insurance didn't cover this pregnancy.

It took forever to get an appointment at the local health

department. I was five months along before I finally saw a doctor.

Just like before, I had gestational diabetes. My blood pressure and blood sugar were dangerously high, and I had to start taking insulin.

My husband treated me like dirt. He couldn't understand that my body was barely holding up. I was exhausted and sick all the time.

One day while he was at work, my son broke a glass. I was so big and weak that I had to crawl to the bathroom because I couldn't walk.

My blood sugar was out of control, and I could barely function. I managed to get the broom, sweep the glass into a corner, and lay the broom over it so my son wouldn't step in it.

When my husband came home, instead of helping, he called me a fat, lazy bitch, threw me on the floor, and rubbed my face in the broken glass, all in front of our little boy, who stood there screaming and crying.

There were so many days like this. He hated me, and I hated him. We were trapped in a marriage neither of us wanted. Sometimes I would leave and go stay at my sister's house for a few days, but I always knew I had to go back.

She couldn't take care of us; she was just a refuge when I needed to escape for a while. She had her own demons to fight at home. I would write to my mother-in-law asking for advice, but wouldn't put too much in the letters because I wouldn't want him to read anything she wrote back.

She would just tell me to be patient and kind and be a good wife. Which sometimes made me want to puke. I felt like she was taking up for him, but I also knew that she didn't know the whole story. Would she react different if I told her everything? I wondered.

I could stay with my other sister sometimes, just to have a place to catch my breath or to watch her girls so she could go out for a bit. She was doing the best she could too, raising two kids on her own and sharing a place with a friend just to make ends meet.

None of us had much during that time. We were all just trying to get through.

So, most days, I stayed where I was and prayed things would somehow get better, because there really wasn't anywhere else to go. They didn't get better. They only got worse.

My pregnancy became so difficult that I had to be hospitalized. My mom came and got my son and kept him while I was there. I stayed in the hospital for almost a month. My husband came to see me once. Just once.

My mother came every weekend and brought my little boy to visit. It was one of the hardest and loneliest times of my life.

When I finally got out, I came home to find that my husband hadn't done anything around the house and hadn't paid a single bill. Just more chaos to deal with.

A few weeks later, my daughter was born, a dark-haired, chubby-cheeked, beautiful baby girl. She was my heart and soul.

The day after she was born, the doctors tied my tubes, and

I can't even describe the relief I felt. For the first time, I knew I would never have to go through another pregnancy with that man again. I was done. And I was glad.

After my daughter was born, I started breastfeeding her, or at least trying to. She would eat, then throw up, eat again, and throw up again.

She wasn't gaining any weight, only losing it. I took her to the doctor several times, and they kept telling me the same thing: it was reflux and that I should try feeding her smaller amounts.

I finally got so frustrated that I took her to my family doctor, the one I had known since I was two years old and who my mother had once worked with.

He ordered an X-ray and discovered that she had pyloric stenosis, a condition where the muscle leading to the stomach closes up, blocking food from passing through. My poor baby had been starving. She was immediately taken in for surgery.

Now that my daughter was finally doing better, I hoped things might settle down for our little family, maybe even get better.

We met another couple; the husband worked at the same place mine did. They had three small children.

Our daughters were only a month apart, our boys were the same age, and they had one older son too. We'd have family barbecues and little get-togethers.

Around them, he was the perfect husband and father. He laughed, helped with the kids, and acted like the man I wished he really was. But as soon as we got home, he turned into someone else entirely.

I used to ask him why he could be so wonderful in front of other people but such an asshole when we were alone. That question always started a fight, a loud, ugly one that I would always lose.

I started spending more time at my sister's house on the weekends. I'd babysit her kids while she went out with friends. I loved those weekends.

My kids and hers played together like siblings, and I loved watching them make memories, laughing, running, just being kids. It gave me a tiny bit of peace.

Of course, he hated it. He accused me of taking his children away from him when he could be spending time with them. I'd remind him that he didn't actually do anything with them, he'd just sit watching Westerns or reading his books.

He'd snap back that it didn't matter what he was doing; they were his children, and he wanted them home. He also didn't want me bringing anyone else's kids over. "I can't afford to feed everyone's kids," he'd grumble, throwing in some rude comment about how my sister should stay home with her own children.

What he never knew was that I cherished those weekends away. They were my only escape, those few hours at my sister's, or even a quiet trip to the laundromat or grocery store. That was the only time I could breathe.

He started hanging out more with his friend from work. I liked spending time with them too, but not every weekend.

Between their three kids and our two, it was loud, chaotic, and exhausting. I didn't want to live like that every weekend. Of course, if I said I didn't want to go, he'd call me a bitch and accuse me of ruining everything for him.

I remember one night so clearly. His friend made a joke about me weighing two hundred pounds, and my husband laughed right along with him. I felt my face burn with humiliation. I had to step outside, just to cry and pull myself together.

That moment was the beginning of the end of our so-called friendship with them. After that, I refused to go along, but he still went, drinking, wasting money, acting single while pretending he wasn't.

All the while, we were living rent-free in my parents' house. One month, he spent so much that we couldn't even pay our light bill, and the electricity was shut off. We ended up staying the night at that same friend's house. I was furious. I'd have rather stayed in the dark at home than sit there pretending everything was fine. But somehow, through it all, he never went without cigarettes. There was always money for those.

Eventually, we moved out of my parents' house, mostly because they were tired of us living there rent-free. Not long after, my parents ended up moving back into that same house when my father changed jobs. I was thankful to have them close again. It felt like a safety net, a place I could go when things got rough. And they did, more often than not.

Me and my husband fought constantly. By then, he had no problem putting his hands on me. He still never hit me straight in the face, but he'd hit me on the side of my head so hard that I'm certain I had a concussion.

He'd kick me, spit on me, yank my hair, and drag me across the room like I was nothing. Worst of all, he didn't care if our toddlers were watching. They would scream and cry, terrified, while he pinned me to the floor. He'd grab my face in his hands, squeezing so tight I could barely breathe, and force me to look at them.

"This is your fault," he'd say. "You're making them cry. You're making me be this way."

And somehow, in those moments, I almost believed him.

At this time, we lived in a tiny rented house. We were poor, maybe bringing in a thousand dollars a month, if that, with two small children still in diapers.

We'd never been on welfare; my parents hadn't used it, and I didn't even know it was an option. We surely would have qualified, though.

It was a Tuesday afternoon, three days till payday. I knew he had about ten dollars left, so I felt confident we could scrape together bread, milk, or a cheap pack of diapers if we needed to.

Then he came home with a new pack of cigarettes and a can of Skoal. He'd blown our last bit of money on his nasty habits. I was furious.

He didn't apologize. He didn't even look at me, just walked past and went outside to mow the yard, like that would spare him from having to face me.

I drove to my mother's and stayed the night, knowing he'd

have to walk to work the next day, his job was close enough that it would only be a half mile or so.

As I pulled away, I saw his glass of tea and the can of Skoal sitting on the truck; they tumbled into the ditch when I left.

The next day I waited inside and watched someone drop him off. He stepped out, cut a switch from a mesquite tree, and came in whipping me with it. I told him to do what he wanted.

I cried and I screamed, but a strange, terrible satisfaction burned under it, I had made him angry, and that anger meant I'd pushed back.

In that moment a little independence was born. I discovered I could endure whatever he threw at me, and I told him, plain as day, that one day he would pay the price for what he had done.

On the outside, to the world, to our friends and family, he looked like a quiet, intelligent man who just didn't have much to say. He came across as a good father.

He was an avid reader, book smart, and always held a job. The problem was, he never made much money, and neither of us knew how to manage what little we had.

Truth is, I was still a teenager on the inside. Barely twenty years old with two babies on my hip, but emotionally I had not moved past fifteen.

I had been tucked beneath his control for four long years, hidden away from everything except him.

My whole identity was centered around surviving him, breathing around his moods, and shaping myself into whatever kept the peace. Outside of giving birth, I had not been allowed to grow. I had not been allowed to become anything.

In my mind, I was still that frightened fifteen-year-old girl he decided to keep for himself, frozen in time while the world kept turning without me.

I was not seen. I was not heard. It was as if the world had forgotten I existed. The only ones who knew I was alive were the two little souls who depended on me.

His mother had written me a letter asking if she could come visit. I was ecstatic and couldn't wait for her to get there.

A few weeks later she was here. It was the best fun week I had in a long time. We spent days just talking and drinking coffee and had pic-nicks outside in the yard with the kids.

One funny thing though, she wasn't very interested in my daughter. I found it strange. She adored my son, but barely paid any attention to the bubbly, happy, smiling six-month-old little girl.

I mean, who doesn't love babies? Of course, my son was adorable too, but you would have thought the love would have been equally shared between the both of them. It was not. And it never was, sad to say.

It was nice for me to have a normal week. He wouldn't be mean to me in front of her. I talked to her about some of the things he had done and again, she gave me advice of being more loving and kinder, once again, not blaming him for anything, or offering to talk to him about his behavior.

This hurt me too, because I thought she loved me and cared for me. How can you listen to someone tell you these things and not get upset? I was baffled.

If I told my mother the truth, she probably would have come to our house and slapped the shit out of him and snatched up me and my kids and took us away from there.

Why is it that I was comfortable enough to tell his mother, but not my own? Why did I tell the one person who wouldn't do anything about it, and not tell those who would have rescued me?

Nobody really knew what I lived with. He was one man in the light and another in the dark. His mother finally moved in with us. She met a man and got married and eventually settled down and became a step-mother to a small child from her husband's previous marriage.

As for me, I lived two lives. The one everyone could see, and the one that kept me awake at night. It's funny at how nobody really knows what goes on behind closed doors.

CHAPTER FOUR: THROUGH THE DOORWAY, TO FREEDOM

The next few years of my life were a whirlwind. We moved so many times I honestly can't remember how many. It was always the same story: we couldn't pay rent, or we got so far behind it was easier to just move somewhere else.

One place in particular still sticks in my mind. It was an old, cold, drafty house, and I hated it. I was scared of it, too.

The house used propane for heat, and I had no experience with heaters like that. We only had one Dearborn heater in the living room, but there were gas valves in every room, easy to turn on with just a twist.

I was constantly checking them, terrified that one of the kids might turn one on and the house would blow sky high.

The house felt lonely, sitting out there in the middle of nowhere. We had no telephone, no cable, this was years before the internet, so as you can imagine, life could get very lonely.

For some reason, he loved everything about this house. The isolation. We only had one vehicle, so I was trapped there day after day. I think he liked it that way, full control of us.

I would write letters back in Alabama to my friends, knowing that I would probably never see them again. It was my way of passing the time during day.

If the kids took a nap, I would sit down and write a letter or two. I only got a few letters back. One time I got one from a friend and she had a baby. The next time I heard about them, she had died in a car wreck. Such sadness between those letters.

I remember telling him about my friend and that she had died. He showed no emotion, almost like he didn't even hear me say it. But hell, he never had any interest in me anyway, why did I think he'd care about one of my friends or what happened to her.

He'd come home from work every day, shower, eat dinner, and then do whatever he wanted. He never asked how our day was or how we were doing.

Most nights he was curled up reading a book. Some people might say, "At least he's home with his family." Maybe they'd be right, except he refused to be disturbed by his family. That was his time, he'd say.

We didn't have conversations unless it was about groceries or something similar. My days were filled with Sesame Street, toddler chatter, cooking meals, and washing clothes.

Sometimes I'd sit on the porch while the kids played, thinking about my friends my age who were in college, living their best young lives. I was trapped, with no life of my own.

One of the only joys outside of my children was going to the grocery store. We had a very limited budget, so I was never in the store long, but he even took that away from me. One day he decided I didn't know how to buy groceries or manage money, so he was going to do the shopping from then on.

One Friday evening he came home from shopping. This is exactly what he bought for our food for the next week: a bag of pinto beans, a bag of rice, a box of oatmeal, a roast, Kool-Aid, tea, coffee, a bag of sugar, and a gallon of milk. I am not joking, this is what he bought for a family of four to eat on for a week, with two toddlers.

As you can imagine, that lasted one whole week, because even his smart mouth was sick of rice and beans by the end of it.

Controlling me was his favorite thing to do. And he excelled at it.

It's not that I didn't love my children. I did. They were my only source of happiness. Their pure little souls meant everything to me. I just needed something more at the young age of twenty-one, to be seen and heard by someone other than my babies.

One night, I pushed him too far. I admit that. He wanted his alone time, and I just wanted a real conversation, something that didn't involve crayons or spilled milk. I was fed up and finally snapped. I stood up and screamed, "Pay attention to me!"

He exploded in a rage I hadn't seen in a long time. He dragged me by my hair down the hallway, sat on top of me, and pressed a knife to my throat. "Leave me alone, your stupid fat bitch," he said, "or I'll cut your fucking throat."

Both of my babies were crying, kneeling beside me, begging him to stop. He stood up and kicked me, screaming, "Look what you made me do in front of my babies! Get up, you stupid bitch!"

It went on for about an hour. Every time one of the kids cried, he'd hit me on the side of my head, telling me it was my fault they were upset. If I cried, he hit me harder, demanding to know what I was crying for. Wasn't this what I wanted? Didn't I start all this just for attention?

There was no right way to respond. Whether I stayed calm or broke down in tears, it only made him angrier. Finally, he yanked me up by my arm and told me to get out of his sight. I pulled myself up and took the kids to their room.

We stayed there the rest of the night.

It was a long, cold night. Usually, we let the kids sleep in our room when it was freezing because it was next to the living room and we kept the door open for heat. But not that night.

I curled up with both of them in one bed and just laid there, wide awake, thinking about what I was about to do.

He was asleep in the next room. His mornings were always the same: he'd sit up, cough, and then light a cigarette.

It was 2 a.m. I crept quietly through the house, double-checking that the Dearborn heater was off, all the way off. Then I turned on every single propane valve in that house.

I loaded my babies into the truck and left.

I drove five miles down the road, knowing in my heart that when he woke up and lit his morning cigarette, he'd blow himself straight into hell.

I felt nothing.

I already had my story planned. I'd tell my parents it was too cold and I'd brought the babies over for the night.

If anyone investigated, they'd just assume one of the kids had turned the valves on. I'd mentioned that fear before.

Nobody would suspect me. Nobody knew what I was living through.

In my mind, it was the perfect plan.

That five-mile drive felt endless.

I don't know how slow I was going, but it felt like an hour. A thousand thoughts went through my head.

Do I keep going or turn around? I wanted to keep driving. I hated him and wanted him out of our lives forever.

Then panic set in.

As much as I hated him, I wasn't a murderer.

I turned around.

When I got back, I was terrified to go inside. I didn't know if he'd heard me leave. I tiptoed onto the porch, listening for any creaking in the floor.

I knew if he was awake, he would be in the living room watching through the windows. He would snatch me by the hair and drag and kick me again.

I was shaking from fear, not the cold, but thank God he was still asleep.

Quietly I turned off all the valves, praying still that he wouldn't wake and catch me.

I tucked my babies back into bed, laid down beside them, and thanked Jesus that he hadn't woken.

I didn't sleep a minute.

That night was my breaking point, my mental breaking point. My trauma had almost caused me to kill my husband.

I knew that the next time something like this happened, one of us might not survive, most likely him.

Once again, we moved, this time from the big drafty house to a small apartment. Mainly because the windows had been blown out by a major storm.

The owners were not concerned with replacing them and it was very hot. We had no air conditioning. It was late spring in Texas, humid, and already very warm.

I was excited to move to town and be closer to people I knew. My best friend lived there, so she could stop by during the day while the asshole was at work.

My mother-in-law lived in the same town too, and she would come by to visit and then take my son back to her house with her. Mostly because she had a little boy around his age, and the two of them could play together.

But even after a few years, the favoritism between my children was still there.

Everyone saw it.

Everyone felt it.

My son called her *my* Nanny.

Not just "Nanny."

Not "Can I go to Nanny's house?"

But "Can I go to *MY* Nanny's house?"

As if somewhere along the way she told him, *"Honey, I am your Nanny. Not everybody else's."*

I know that may sound crazy to some people. But it was noticeable. It was there. It was in the tone. In the possessiveness of it. And I wasn't the only one who picked up on it, other people commented on it too.

Meanwhile, my daughter just called her "Nanny."

Plain and simple.

No claim.

No special title.

No ownership.

And even though nobody ever said anything out loud, you could feel the difference.

I'm sure my daughter felt the difference too, but she was truly a Moma's girl and that was ok.

My mother, her granny, loved her deeply and thought she was such a beautiful child. Truthfully, my mother was one of the only people my daughter would stay with.

I knew she felt that true maternal feeling that radiated within her. My mother-in-law did not have that. Maybe that's why she was better with boys/men than girls/women.

In the attempt to try and loose some weight, I started exercising with one of my lifelong family friends. The kids and I would go over in the evenings and walk with her.

Having girl time was like a gift from God. I enjoyed that time every day. I started losing some weight and, to be honest, my husband was starting to pay a little bit of attention to me.

He still didn't really do much with us, but with a small social life I didn't rely on him anymore for conversation.

One evening I was going to do my walk. I asked him if the kids could stay home with him and give me some alone time. He did not take this well.

He wanted to know why I needed alone time. I explained that I very seldom got to do anything alone and it would be nice from time to time.

Once again, he exploded. This time he accused me of seeing someone, that I must not be going walking but going to sleep with someone else.

Another big fight. He told the kids to go to their room, and they did immediately. He took me to our bedroom and started yelling and cussing me out, saying horrible things and hitting me in the side of the head as usual.

I swear I have head trauma from this, years of being hit on the side of the head.

I sat there and listened. I was used to it. I'd learned to hold my head down because I didn't want him to see my tears anymore. I didn't want him to know that he was physically and mentally hurting me. I was becoming stronger, but I didn't know it. I guess he needed a cigarette and couldn't find his lighter.

He left the bedroom to go to the kitchen to light his cigarette on the stove. I waited for him to round the corner to the kitchen and I ran *through the doorway* and outside.

I knew he wouldn't chase me, because he didn't dare act this way in public. I ran to a phone and called my mother to come get me.

When my mother arrived, all she knew was that we had a fight and I needed to come stay with her for a night or two.

Something in me caught a glimpse of independence and I didn't want to go back. During those two weeks, I visited my friends and discussed how I would manage living on my own and going to work. I didn't have a car, a high school diploma, or money. I was pretty much on my own.

My parents were struggling financially during that time and couldn't take care of us either. Well, they could, but I didn't want to lay that on them.

I remember one night I was going to take the kids over to the apartment to drop them off for the night to see him. I used my mom's car to go over there.

He was very charming to me, asked me to come inside and talk. He kissed the kids and asked them to go play in their room for a minute while we talked.

He looked at me and told me it was time for me to come home. I told him that I was tired of the way our life was and how I had no life other than the kids. He did not take this very well.

He immediately got upset. I saw that he was getting angry and I headed for the door. He slammed it shut, not allowing me to leave.

He was telling me how stupid I was and that nobody was ever going to have my fat ass, gritting through his teeth while talking to me. I yanked the door open and said, "We'll see about that."

He grabbed for me, but I made my way out. I got in the car, shaking so bad I could barely drive. This was one of the only times I had ever really stood up to him.

And oh my God, it felt wonderful.

I went over to my friend's house afterwards, and I will never forget that night. We laughed, we joked about school and old memories, and for the first time in a long time, I felt like my own person again.

It was one of those rare moments when the sun breaks through even the darkest clouds, reminding you that there is still something bright behind the darkness.

I had been lost for so many years, wandering without a map, not even sure which direction led home. But that night, I could finally see a little light again.

At the end of those two weeks, it was clear I couldn't make it on my own. As bad as I wanted to, it just wasn't time yet.

My parents weren't very supportive, but to be fair, they didn't know the whole story. I was too ashamed to tell them everything. So, to them, it looked like we were just having a normal married-people fight.

They encouraged me to go back home, which was their way of saying they weren't going to help me start over.

So, I went back.

But I didn't go back the same.

I went back with the threat that if he ever laid a hand on me again, I would leave and never come back. And for a long time, he didn't hit me.

He still talked ugly. Still called me names when he got mad. But the fear of losing me, of losing the kids, of paying child support, kept him in line just enough to look like progress.

His mother treated me differently after that time apart. I could feel it. She was going to take his side no matter what. She knew what he was doing. She knew who he was. But somehow, I was the one not being a good enough wife.

Her advice, once again, was the same tired script:

Keep the house clean.
Cook him good meals.
Don't nag.
Let him be.

I wanted to say,
Oh, and take the ass beatings when he gets mad too, right?

But of course, I didn't.

I just nodded.

Because when you're young, scared, broke, and ashamed, you learn really quick how to swallow your own voice just to survive the day.

We moved to another town that was closer to his job. I had started babysitting for a friend and I would also clean houses for extra money.

My mother had found an old word processor at a garage sale for $10 and she bought it for me. I have always wanted to be writer. I mainly did poems, but have always known that I wanted to write a novel.

He would make fun of me when I asked for him to tend to the kids so I could go and write for a while. He would just chuckle as if I was stupid to say something like that. But to me, it was my little dream, and I enjoyed doing it so screw what he thought about it.

I remember one early summer night; we had just finished eating dinner. It was a Tuesday around 8pm and I saw headlights pull in the driveway.

It was odd for somebody to be at our house on a Tuesday night at eight o'clock. We never got company past five or six in the evening.

I peeked my head out the window and saw that it was my dad. He was the only one who got out, Mom stayed in the truck. I opened the door, and Dad walked in with a strange look on his face.

"What's up?" I asked.

He said, "Let's go in here. I've got some news to tell you."

My husband got up and followed us into the kitchen. Dad looked at me and said that my sister had been killed in a car wreck, and they were on their way down there to pick up her kids.

I screamed and grabbed my face, crying so hard I could barely breathe. My husband just stood there, staring at me like an idiot. Out of the corner of my eye, I saw my dad nudge him, telling him, without words, to put his arms around me.

It was like he had to be told to comfort me, as if the thought wouldn't come naturally. His wife was breaking down right in front of him, and he had absolutely no desire to reach out or show me any kind of love or comfort.

The next few months were sad and depressing. My mother slipped into a deep depression, and we had my sister's kids pretty much all the time. If they weren't at Mom and Dad's, they were at my house, which upset my husband greatly.

He said, "We're not going to take on the responsibility of these kids. It's not my damn fault your sister died."

I hated him for saying that. I hated the way he talked about her, and the way he felt about my nieces, two little girls who no longer had a mother.

Neither of them had a relationship with their fathers, and since they were born, I had helped take care of them. Part of me felt like I was their mother. But he didn't want any part of that.

After a few months, things slowly started to fall back into their normal rhythm. My mom went back to work. I would keep the girls while she worked, and one morning

I noticed something strange. It was five o'clock, and she was supposed to drop them off, but instead of stopping, she just drove right past my house. Then she turned around, came back, and pulled into the driveway.

I went out to meet her and said, "What's going on? I saw you drive by."

She was acting off. Her face didn't look right, and she wasn't talking clearly. It scared me, but she insisted on going to work that day.

That evening, she came back to pick up the girls, and we both knew something was wrong. She went to the doctor and found out she had suffered a mini-stroke.

That was just the beginning.

Over the next year, she had several more, some large ones that changed everything about her. She had to relearn how to talk, eat, bathe, and walk steadily again. It was a complete and total nightmare, one that seemed to never end.

During all of this, my husband had moments where he acted decent, but that was mostly because he respected my mother.

He admired her strength as a woman and a parent, and he felt sorry for what she was going through after my sister's death.

But when it became clear that Mom wasn't going to get better, and I was constantly over there helping or taking care of my sister's kids, it became a bigger and bigger issue between us.

The next year rolled around, and I was still helping take care of my mom. She was doing better, though. I still went out there every few days, but she was getting along pretty well on her own.

I had gotten a job at a local convenience store as the night manager. I was proud of that position. Some people might have just seen me as a cashier, but I knew

I had real responsibility, and I genuinely enjoyed the work. My coworkers were good people, and I loved the sense of independence that came with it.

I had no idea at the time that this job would change the way I saw myself. It showed me what I was capable of, and for the first time in a long time, I felt like me.

As fate would have it, all the heavy lifting, stocking coolers, unloading trucks, moving boxes, caught up with me. I developed a hernia in my lower abdomen, and my gallbladder became badly inflamed. I ended up needing surgery for both at once.

A few nights before my surgery, my girlfriends from work wanted to have a little farewell party for me since I'd be out for about six weeks.

We had a few drinks and went to a get-together where some of our other friends were hanging out. A few of the guys my husband worked with were there too, and they made sure to tell him the next day that I had been at that party.

When my husband got home from work, he dragged me into the bedroom, furious. He started yelling, saying how embarrassed he was to have such a "whore" for a wife.

I tried to walk out of the room, but he slammed the door shut and locked it. Then he grabbed me by the hair, dragged me to the bathroom, and shoved my head into the toilet, demanding I tell him who I had slept with that night.

He knew I hadn't done anything. I had only spent a few hours laughing and talking with my girlfriends, but that didn't matter. I ended up on my knees, begging him to stop. I apologized over and over, telling him I was sorry, that I was a bad wife, just to get him to calm down.

That was the atmosphere I was in when I went in for surgery two days later. He didn't come to the hospital. My mom and dad did. I saw him the next day, and he barely said a word to me.

A few weeks after surgery, things took a turn for the worse when I developed a staph infection called MRSA. I got so sick that I had to be placed in isolation and was in and out of the hospital for months.

During that time, one of my friends from the store helped my husband get the kids to and from school and daycare, or at least that's what I thought she was doing. Turns out, she was "helping" him with other things, if you catch my drift.

She swore nothing happened between them, but she was so full of guilt that she had to confess something. To this day, I'm not exactly sure what she was confessing to, but my husband didn't deny a thing.

I told him that as soon as I was fully recovered, I'd be divorcing him. Until then, I expected him to take care of the kids and the house. And when I got better, really better, I did exactly what I said I would. I went back to work, asked him to move out, and he did.

I have never in my life felt such a glorious feeling as I did that day.

Even though him moving out felt glorious, I guess he figured that meant he didn't have to take care of anything anymore. So, there I was, paying all the bills, buying groceries, and taking care of the kids, all on my little convenience store salary. He had pretty much abandoned us and taken the only car we had.

My mom ended up giving me her car since she couldn't drive anymore, and I was so thankful for that. At least I had a way to get around without worrying about a car payment.

Months went by, and I had no idea where he was. His mother refused to tell me anything, and the only way I could reach him was through his job.

Finally, me and my best friend decided to do a little detective work of our own. I had to go pick up the kids from his mother's house and while she stepped out of the room, I looked at her caller ID on her phone.

I pretty much knew everyone who called her, so I wrote down the ones I didn't know and then we looked them all up in the phone book.

What we found out made my stomach turn, he was living with the woman who owned the daycare where my daughter went while I was at work. What a surprise.

He had moved in with a woman whose family had money. Not only was he not helping us, but he was living somewhere where he didn't have to pay a single bill. He had taken the vehicle that I bought and paid for and traded it in for a four-wheel drive truck.

He didn't even need a four-wheel drive. I guess he thought it made him look tough. He always wanted to be a cowboy, well, now he had his big old truck.

It made me laugh.
And it made me sick all at the same time.

I knew one day karma would get him. He was a phony, a fake. I knew the real monster he was, even if no one else did. I also knew that sooner or later, other people would see it too.

And she did.
Eventually, she asked him to leave.

It took about a year for me to fully heal from the surgery I'd gone through. After developing the staph infection, I had to go back in for multiple surgeries.

All of this happened while he was living with the other woman. When she finally threw him out, he moved back in with his mother for a while.

Not long after that, I got sick again and needed help. So, he moved back in, but we lived separate lives under the same roof. I stayed in the main bedroom, and he slept in my daughter's room. We didn't talk, didn't eat together, didn't share anything. He handled the house and the kids in the evenings, and I did what I could during the day.

I couldn't work; I had an IV in my arm that I had to take home with me. Recovery was slow, painful, and exhausting.

The kids spent a lot of time with his mother. And I'll say this: she was a good nanny in the practical sense.

They were fed, they were safe, they were watched. But the difference in how she treated my children, that was something else entirely.

She was overly attached to my son. It was unsettling at times, like she wanted him for herself. My daughter she didn't mistreat outright, not in the way people expect when they hear the word cruel, but she targeted her. Small things. Intentional things. Always noticeable.

While he was living back in the house, I got a phone call. I was in the bedroom and answered it there. He was in the kitchen making coffee and saw the caller ID, it was my doctor.

He thought that was strange that the doctor was calling me at home. Truthfully, this doctor and I had a long history at that point, I had almost died during that surgery mess, and I believe he was showing me extra attention and calling to checkup on me to keep me from suing him.

When I walked into the kitchen, he asked why a doctor would be calling me at home. I said, "To check on me. To make sure I'm okay."

He looked at me and said, "Oh, yeah...I "bet" he is."

That was all it took.

I told him to fuck off.

He couldn't hit me, not then. I was too fragile. Too many stitches. Too many wounds. But he still found a way to hurt me.

He cussed me out in front of the kids, grabbed the pot of fresh coffee, and poured it straight across my stomach, on top of the staples from my surgery.

The pain was instant. Blinding. But worse than the pain was what my daughter saw.
She was right there.
And she still remembers it to this day.

Because that wasn't just physical pain.
That was *the kind that rearranges a child's entire understanding of love and safety.*

Once I got healed and things started getting back to normal, I went back to work. We worked out an arrangement and I got an apartment just down the street, and we shared custody of the kids. It wasn't ideal, but it was what I had to do at the time.

He worked a steady Monday-through-Friday schedule, while mine was all over the place, some weeknights and usually one or two nights on the weekend. We made it work the best we could.

Life went on like that for a while. I can't even fully remember if he decided to move out of our house because he didn't want to live there anymore or if he moved in with his girlfriend, but eventually, he moved out, so I moved back in.

It seemed as though he just walked out one day. He left a lot of his things behind, clothes, boxes, random stuff shoved into a closet.

We hadn't set up an official custody schedule yet because the divorce wasn't final. I had already filed, but it was still dragging along. When the court date finally came, he didn't even show up. There really wasn't much to divide between us anyway, just the kids and child support. Since he wasn't there to contest anything, I got what I asked for.

It took forever for the child support to actually start, though, and in the meantime, I was struggling to make ends meet. I was trying to keep the house going by myself, working, and taking care of the kids.

At one point, the back door broke and I couldn't get it fixed. It became a big issue. I came home one day to find a stray dog running around inside my house; a major sign that it was time to move. I couldn't handle this on my own anymore.

Not long after that, a friend of mine asked if I wanted to get a place with her. It made sense at the time, two single moms trying to help each other out, so that's what we did.

I left all of his stuff that he had left behind in that closet. It probably wasn't the right thing to do, but I didn't care one tiny bit about him or his things. I left them there for that stray dog to have, seemed fitting.

I had finally gotten what I wanted, away from him. Even though I was still struggling financially, I finally had peace. I didn't have to worry about being criticized, humiliated, or hurt anymore. All I had to focus on was taking care of my children.

The ten years of misery and hate were over. I was free of him and he no longer had control of me or my life. I survived.

I worked multiple jobs at a time just to make ends meet. There were stretches when things got so tight that I had to move back in with my parents for a while. It wasn't easy, but it was safe. And for the first time in a long time, that was enough.

Once we got into the swing of our custody schedule, I started having a little time to myself. For the first time in years, I could breathe.

That space gave me the chance to figure out who I was and to experience things I had never been able to before, like dating.

I wouldn't even say my husband and I ever really dated. One weekend I met him, and a couple of months later I was living in his house.

So actually, going out with someone, getting to know them, and deciding for myself whether I liked them or not was a brand-new experience.

It was nice to be able to go out for a drink with my girlfriends, have a conversation with a guy, and realize that I had a choice.

If I wasn't interested, I could simply turn around and walk away. That felt strange at first, but also kind of amazing and liberating.

I had found my freedom, but it didn't always look or feel the way I expected.

Maybe I had escaped the big bad wolf, but sometimes the wolves came dressed as sheep.

CHAPTER FIVE: LEARNING TO STAND ON MY OWN

I was discovering that all my newfound freedom was anything but peaceful. It felt like standing in the middle of a quiet room with the air knocked out of me, trying to remember how to breathe.

People talk about leaving like it is the ending. The victory. The rescue. But leaving was only the first step. The true work came afterward. Hell, it came for years to come. The part nobody warns you about.

The part where you wake up every morning and realize that no one else is steering the ship anymore. I had gone from being controlled to being fully responsible. That kind of shift will shake a person to their bones.

I was raising two children alone. Working full time. Paying every bill. Constantly robbing Peter to pay Paul, and still not making ends meet. Making every meal. Folding laundry late at night and waking up before the sun.

And on top of that, I was helping my mother and my nieces

because life keeps moving even when you are exhausted. I did not have the luxury of falling apart. I did not even have the luxury of sitting still. I just kept going because if I stopped for too long everything might collapse.

Healing did not feel gentle. It did not feel quiet. It felt like a fight. And not against him anymore. A fight against myself. Against the fears he planted in me. Against the memories that found me when the house was finally still.

At night came the dreams, the bad, ugly dreams. They felt real. He was always there in them. Not as a memory but as a presence. I would dream of him blocking doorways. Taking my keys. Holding me down.

Speaking in that cruel, cold voice and always gritting his teeth. I would wake up, heart racing, sheets soaked, shaking like he was still right there in the room with me.

I would lie still in the dark, listening, making sure the house was safe, reminding myself that I was free. It took years for those dreams to stop. Some nights they still visit.

People think trauma ends when you leave. But that's not how it works. Trauma follows you. It lingers in the corners of your mind, becomes the lens you see yourself through, the voice you still answer to without realizing it.

You know that feeling, like something's following you down the hallway at night? That's not a ghost- that's trauma. That's PTSD. It's the fear you've carried for so long it's learned your name.

And when the hair stands up on the back of your neck, it's

not the dead reaching for you. It's the past, reminding you it's still there.

And it did not just show up in my sleep. It showed up in my choices.

There were jobs I quit because the stress felt too familiar. Because the moment someone raised their voice at me, I felt that old panic rise and I ran.

There were times I packed up and moved when life got heavy because running felt safer than staying put. I changed towns like most people change hairstyles. If I could not control the pain, I could at least change the scenery.

And relationships. Lord. I chose men who mirrored what I believed I deserved. If a man was kind to me, I felt suspicious. If he was emotionally unavailable, I felt drawn in. If he was controlling, I felt like I already knew the rules.

I did not believe I deserved tenderness.

I did not believe I was someone worth loving. I believed I was used up. Damaged. Too heavy in body and too heavy in spirit. I believed my history was written all over me. I believed no man would ever want a woman who had come from that kind of hell.

So, I settled for less. Again, and again. Because I thought that is who I was. A woman with baggage. A woman who survived but never fully healed. A woman who was grateful for crumbs.

I want to tell you it changed overnight, but it did not. Healing did not come in one big moment.

It came in the quiet. In the small hours. In the slow rebuilding of my sense of self. Over decades.

I rebuilt myself little by little. Not in triumph. Not in big steps. But in tiny moments no one else ever saw.

Freedom did not feel strong at first. It felt fragile. It felt uncertain. It felt like a newborn fawn trying to stand on legs that had never held weight before.

But those legs held.

And so, did I.

Even before I fully knew who I was becoming

I knew who I was not anymore.

And that was the beginning.

There was no single day when I woke up healed. No moment where everything suddenly made sense. It was more like learning to live all over again.

I was growing up at the same time I was raising children.

I was learning how to make choices that came from me instead of fear. Some days I did well. Some days I just survived.

But every day I was building something. A life. A home. A version of myself that was not defined by what had been done to me. I did not realize it then, but those years were the foundation.

The slow, steady work of learning how to exist in my own skin.

The beginning of coming back to myself. I wrote something one night, long before I had language for my healing.

It poured out of me before I understood what it meant. I understand it now.

> A drink of wine at the end of the day
> No longer give a damn what you have to say
> Knowing my life is my own-
> My way
> And you didn't leave me
> I escaped-
> Never think I cried for you
> I cried for me
> I learned the truth
> Forgiving you is half the equation
> Forgiving myself is liberation
> See me babe
> See me wave
> You didn't leave me
> I escaped-

This is the voice of the woman who lived.
And she is still here.

CHAPTER SIX: THAT WHICH DOES NOT KILL US

Another year was coming to an end. Just a couple of months left, and I found myself working full-time at a good job but living with my parents. It was simpler that way.

Mom could help with the kids since I had to be up early for work. She would get them off to school in the mornings, and I'd be there in the evenings when they got home.

It worked for us. We were happy. The kids loved living at my mom's because it felt safe and stable. Nobody fought. They had the woods to play in, building forts out there like I used to when I was little. All the neighbors were people I'd known my whole life, and there was comfort in that.

The kids would go to their Nanny's house at times too, mostly my son, because of course he was her favorite. My daughter preferred to stay with my mom or go to my sister's house with the other little girls in the family.

I spent a lot of time with one of my girlfriends who also had kids. One Friday afternoon, we picked our children up from school after the high school pep rally. My daughter was wearing her little cheerleader uniform, so proud and excited.

The plan was simple: drop my friend off to meet her boyfriend and then head back for the football game with the kids.

But on the way back, everything changed.

We had a major blowout, and the car flipped end over end three times. I was thrown out the windshield. My two children were thrown out the side and back windows. And my friend's beautiful daughter, sitting in the front seat, was killed instantly when the corner of the vehicle struck her in the head.

Life as I knew it changed in an instant.

I found my children lying in ditches, and for a moment, I thought they were dead. I ran to the car and saw my friend's daughter, and knew right away she was gone. I went into shock.

It's hard to explain that feeling... I felt nothing, yet everything, all at once.

I went back to my children and waited till the ambulance arrived. My daughter drifted in and out of consciousness, and my son, thank God, seemed to be okay.

He had some cuts and bruises, but he was conscious and talking. My children were sent to separate hospitals, and by some miracle, we made it through with only a concussion and a broken pinky toe between them.

To say that angels were protecting my children is an

understatement. In my heart, I believe that at the moment my friend's daughter died, her spirit stayed behind to protect my two kids, to make sure they lived.

Some people might call that emotion or imagination, but unless you've lived through something like that, you have no right to judge what I believe.

I remember how my ex-husband treated me when he arrived at the hospital. Immediate hate and blame from him. I never said one word to him, not one.

He and his mother went to the hospital with my son and I went to the other hospital with my daughter. I called multiple times to check up on my son- but they never called once to check on my daughter. Not once.

For months and months after the accident, I lived with unbearable guilt. I replayed it over and over in my mind, trying to make sense of it.

I've had plenty of flat tires in my life, but never one that made me lose control the way that one did. I wasn't even driving fast; we were only going about sixty miles an hour when it happened.

Eventually, we found out that a part of the car was defective, and worse, that the manufacturer had known about it. That defect caused the tire failure and the loss of control that led to the crash. It made headlines across the country, but none of that changed how I felt.

Knowing the truth didn't erase the pain. It didn't bring her back. It didn't quiet the guilt that sat like a heavy stone in my gut. All it left me with was a whole lot of nothingness inside.

It didn't take long for everyone around us to realize that this meant a lawsuit. The details of it were sealed, and we weren't supposed to talk about any of it.

But without spilling the beans, I can say this much: my children's hospital bills were taken care of, and that was about it.

My friend, who had lost her daughter, was awarded much more, and that was completely fine with me. I didn't want money. It felt like blood money, and I didn't want a single penny of it.

But people love to talk, and word spread fast. Before long, folks in town and the surrounding areas started whispering that I was going to get rich off that wreck.

That couldn't have been further from the truth. I didn't get rich, not even close. But that rumor brought out a whole new kind of trouble. Which brings me back to the wolves in sheep's clothing.

Let's talk about sheep number one.

He was a local guy, kind of cute, funny, and his parents were outstanding members of the community. He was a recovering alcoholic and, as far as I knew, he had been sober for a while.

He didn't have much, but I didn't care. I had so much fun just sitting around and talking with him. He made me laugh in ways I had not laughed in years.

We would get in his Jeep and ride through the country, talking and listening to music. I could be myself with him completely.

And honestly, he was not the best-looking guy, but that did

not matter. What mattered was how easy it felt to just *be*.

But boy, oh boy, did he have an ulterior motive.

We dated for a few months. He would come around and joke with the kids, and they thought he was just someone helping out.

Every time he came over, he fixed something. One time it was a hole in the wall, another time it was a light fixture. In their minds, he was simply the man who fixed things.

I never introduced him as anything more than his name. He was not around them much, only here and there. And he never stayed the night when they were home, only when they were with their dad.

It was on one of those fun Jeep rides that he suddenly seemed to get quiet and sad out of nowhere. I asked him what was wrong, and he just said, "Oh, nothing. I don't want to bother you with it."

We'd gotten to that point in the relationship where, of course, I cared and wanted to know what was on his mind. Looking back now, I can see exactly what he was doing, setting me up to ask.

And I did. I said, "No, babe, what's wrong? You can tell me. I want to help."

That's when he started telling me that he was having some financial problems, that money had been tight, and it just weighed heavy on him sometimes.

Me, being poor as dirt myself, never once thought he'd look at me as someone who had anything to give. But of course, I wanted to understand and help, so I dug a little deeper. I asked what was going on, how bad it was, and if there was anything I could do.

He said he'd been having trouble with back taxes and needed about $10,000 to pay them off or he was going to get into serious trouble.

I actually chuckled when he said it and asked, "Do you honestly think I have that kind of money?"

The second the words left my mouth; I saw it all over his face, that moment of realization. That was when he figured out, I didn't have what he was after. He mentioned the lawsuit.

I told him the truth, plain and simple: I got just enough money to pay my kids' hospital bills, and that was it. "I don't have money to give anybody," I said. "If I did, I would-but I don't."

You could *feel* the air change. It was like I had just taken all the wind out of his sails. Everything shifted in that moment. He pulled the Jeep over, reached into a little pouch he carried, and pulled out a joint.

Then he sat there and got high right in front of me, something he had never done before. So even his soberness was not real. He just found a different method to fuel his habit.

I knew then that I was his last hope. And I also knew, deep down, that this was probably the last time I would see him. I wasn't someone he truly wanted. I was just someone he thought he could get money from.

Days went by, and I didn't hear from him. I called a few times, but he never answered. I left a couple of messages, and still-nothing.

Finally, one day I decided to drive by his house. I caught him off guard, mostly because I wanted to make him face me. He gave me some vague excuse, saying he was "just going through some things" and that it wasn't personal.

But I knew better. I knew exactly what he'd expected from me.

Looking back now, I'm actually thankful I didn't have that kind of money to give him. I can't help but wonder how long he would've dragged it out, how long he would've pretended to care just to justify taking $10,000 from me.

The Lord really does work in mysterious ways.

Time went on. I worked a couple of different jobs and moved a few times, and somehow, I ended up living with my parents again.

To say I'd had a lot of ups and downs would be putting it mildly.

There were days I wondered if I'd ever crawl out of the funk my life seemed stuck in. Honestly, deep down, I felt like I'd already suffered enough, between my marriage, the abuse, and the car wreck.

I kept hoping that maybe, just maybe, some kind of light would finally break through all that darkness. I remember one time a boss of mine told me that it seemed like our family was cursed.

That stayed with me and haunted me for years.

Maybe they were right, because then came another blow.

It was Christmas Day. I woke up to my dad knocking on my

door, his voice tense. "Get up," he said. "We need to go to your brother's house.

He tried to kill himself last night. Shot himself in the face. He's still alive. They took him to the hospital. I need to go get his truck and his guns."

That's how I woke up on Christmas morning.

Thank God my children were at their dad's house. They'd spent Christmas Eve with me and were supposed to spend Christmas Day with him. So, I got dressed-numb and shaking-and went with my dad.

We arrived at my brother's place first. The scene was... something I'll never forget. It was gruesome, like something you can't ever unsee.

Then we drove to the hospital, and somehow, that was even worse. There he was, lying in the bed, half of his face gone, barely hanging on to life.

All I could focus on was my poor mother. She had already been through so much, losing my sister, and now this. Now she had to face watching her son fight for his life after trying to take it.

It would take months upon months of recovery. Everyone had to adjust their lives to help him heal and to keep things going.

But somehow, we all pulled together and did what needed to be done.

Eventually, I moved out and found a place of my own so my brother could move in with Mom. She took care of him the best she could, and I knew that was where he needed to be.

I had gotten a new job at a car dealership. To be honest, I basically lied on my application-said I knew how to use a fax machine, operate a multi-line phone, and work on a personal computer. The truth was, I didn't know how to do any of that.

But I knew one thing for sure: I had to get a steady Monday-through-Friday; eight-to-five job if I wanted to be a better mother to my children.

The man who interviewed me had once been a psychology professor at a university, and the dealership was kind of his retirement gig.

He told me later that he hired me because he fell in love with my personality. He said I reminded him of his daughter, determined, a little rough around the edges, but full of heart.

He taught me everything he knew about the car business, and before long, I found my rhythm. It turned out to be a good, steady career, and for the first time in a long time, I started to feel proud of myself again.

One day after work, I stopped by the grocery store. I was standing in line, flipping through one of the magazines on the end rack, when something caught my eye. Right there on the front cover was a story about my car wreck.

My heart dropped.

As I waited in line, I opened the magazine and started to read, and there it was, words that I had said to my friend in the hospital after her daughter died.

My *words.* Printed in black and white for the whole world to see.

I was mortified. Nobody had ever interviewed me. Nobody had asked permission. Nobody had even called. I felt sick to my stomach.

I left the store right then and there, my cart full of groceries still sitting in the checkout line.

I called my attorney as soon as I got to my car and demanded to know what was going on. He told me that my friend, the mother of the little girl who died, had been doing interviews.

By that time, she and I had already drifted apart. The grief was too much for both of us; it was awkward and painful to even look at each other.

But I never imagined she'd start giving interviews and talking about something that was still ripping both our hearts out.

And then came the rumors.

In a small town, you don't even have to sneeze before people start talking. Word spread fast, ugly, twisted rumors that I had been drunk that day and had let her daughter drive because I couldn't.

People I had known my entire life actually believed it.

Never mind that we had just left a pep rally and it was only four in the afternoon. Never mind that I barely drink now and didn't drink at all back then.

Even when I went out with friends, one beer was about my limit. I've never been a drinker.

But some fool decided to make up a story, and people ran with it-that she died because I was drinking and let her drive.

Which was ridiculous, because anyone who knows the law knows that after any fatal accident, the driver is automatically tested for drugs and alcohol. I was tested. I was clean.

Still, that didn't stop the whispers. Because, well... that's how it goes in a small town.

That year, when I got my income tax return, I ended up with a decent lump sum. With two small children, it came out to a few thousand dollars. It might not sound like much, but to me, it was everything.

I decided to move out of town, to a place where nobody knew me, nobody knew about the car wreck, nobody thought I had money, and nobody knew anything about my horrible marriage. I just wanted a fresh start.

At the time, I had been seeing a man who had recently gone through a divorce. I was head over heels in love with him, but deep down, I knew he didn't feel the same way about me.

Still, he helped me move, and for that, I was grateful.

We settled in a small town, and for a while, things were okay. But after a few months, I could see it in my kids' faces, they were sad.

They didn't know anyone, and they were still carrying the weight of everything we'd already been through. About six months in, I realized they just weren't adjusting. They needed home.

So, I made the decision to move back. By that time, the lawsuit had finally been settled, all the medical bills had been paid, and I had about $10,000 left over from the settlement. I used that money to buy a mobile home, a place that would finally be ours.

I always thought it was funny, in a twisted kind of way, that I ended up with about $10,000 left over-the exact amount that idiot had wanted from me.

It was almost poetic. The same money he tried to manipulate me for was the money I ended up using to build a new life for me and my kids. God really does have a way of flipping the script sometimes.

I asked my sister if she wanted to come live with me so we could get a trailer house together and make one big, happy family. She said yes, and we went out and picked one together.

We lasted about two years under the same roof. Amazingly, we survived without killing each other, but barely. Sisters will be sisters.

Looking back now, I have no idea what we were thinking, but at the time, it felt like the right thing to do. We had good intentions, though, and despite the chaos, I still love her dearly to this day.

I was still sort of seeing the guy I'd met before I moved. There were times when he seemed genuinely concerned, caring, kind, and interested in me, and then there were other times when he didn't. Looking back, I think maybe he just wanted someone to help look after his daughter.

He'd gotten custody of her in the divorce, and she was a young teenager who needed a lot of guidance. I tried to be there for her as much as I could.

I cared deeply about both of them, especially him. I know he never meant to break my heart, but he did. And it left a very deep scar.

I wouldn't call him a wolf in sheep's clothing, because he wasn't. He did a lot of good things for me and helped me in ways I'll always appreciate.

But we both let it go on longer than we should have. I got too attached, and it became another battle scar, another wound on a heart that already had too many.

I don't hold any ill will toward him. I just wish we had stayed friends instead of trying to make a relationship work. I think, maybe, that would've lasted longer.

Time slipped by the way it does. I met a couple of other men, both of which were disasters.

Jobs came and went; in the car business, it's always up and down. I ended up losing the mobile home. It was repossessed, and I was once again living with my parents. My brother had moved into a house of his own once he had recuperated from his surgeries.

I worked at a local dealership and life was good. My niece was also living with us. She was in high school and had been through an emotional and physical rollercoaster of her own with her biological father, and ended up living with Mom and Dad full-time.

Which is where she and her sister should have always been since their mother's death. But some idiotic judge gave custody to their two deadbeat dads after my sister's passing.

I was at work one cold January morning, and I got a phone call from my mother. She couldn't breathe. I hung up and left immediately and took her to the ER.

Within a couple hours she was taken by ambulance to a bigger hospital a couple hours away. I called Dad, who was out of town working, and told him to come home right away.

We arrived at the hospital, and Mom was in the cardiac ICU- the main artery in her heart was torn. It was very serious. The doctor said if she made it through the night, we would transfer her to Galveston to the heart hospital.

We all went in to see Mom. Her children and husband surrounded her bed. I always had a close relationship with Mom. We had very similar sense of humors.

She was very nauseous due to the heart issues, and she kept gagging. In our funny way, I looked at her and said, "Mom, you gotta stop. If you throw up, I will throw up, then everyone will throw up." She started laughing, and so did everyone else.

At that moment, the nurse came in and gave Mom a dose of Phenergan nausea medication through her IV, which knocked her out almost immediately. So, the family stepped outside to let her rest.

Mom died in her sleep. Her last memory was of her husband and children joined and laughing with her. A beautiful way to end a life.

My mother was dead at the age of 58.

A very hard blow to our family. She was the heart of the family-always had been. How do I live a life without my mother in it? I left the hospital, got in my car, and drove around until daylight. I didn't want to go to my home. The home she built. The home she raised me in. But I had to.

I still had Dad, who had been with my mom since grade school. Their whole lives were side by side. How would he manage without her?

And also, my nieces. They had already lost their mother, and now their grandmother-a main sense of stability since birth.

My ex-husband, who once loved and admired my mother, never sent a card, did not come to the funeral or even acknowledge that she passed away.

But his mother did - she met me outside afterwards, hugged me and said, "I will be your mother now." I almost slapped her.

She said it in a tone that almost meant I didn't have a choice. If only she could hear the thoughts in my mind. Maybe she could read it in my eyes, I know they were speaking loudly.

But now it was time to focus on my dad and my nieces. I needed to step up and be a better daughter and aunt.

A much bigger task than I could ever imagine.

CHAPTER SEVEN: EDUCATION IS POWER

After Mom died, we all struggled to put life back together. Dad went through a grieving period that took him to a place I had never seen before. One memory from that first spring stands out clear as day.

It was storm season , the kind where the sky turns that strange green and the air gets still. Tornado warnings were buzzing on the TV.

I was rounding up the kids, telling them to get in the bathtub like we'd always been taught. I kept calling for Dad to come with us, but he didn't answer.

I stepped out of the bathroom and ran down the hallway. The house was quiet. When I looked out the front door, I saw him standing in the driveway, looking straight up into the storm. It reminded me of Lieutenant Dan in *Forrest Gump*, sitting in his wheelchair on that shrimp boat during the hurricane, yelling and laughing hysterically at the storm.

Except Dad wasn't laughing.

He looked like he was daring the storm to take him. And I believe, in that moment, he would have welcomed it. It had only been a few months since Mom passed, and his depression was heavy and deep.

I didn't know how to help him. I just kept the kids safe and waited for the thunder to pass, outside and inside our home.

But as summer came around, something in him started to shift. My niece stepped up and became his companion in a way none of us expected.

She cooked for him, cleaned the house, made sure he ate. She kept him grounded. That gave me a little peace.

So, when the time felt right, I started looking for a place for me and the kids. By mid, summer, we moved into a small apartment in town. It wasn't fancy, but it was ours. A new beginning in the middle of a storm-torn year.

I wanted a career this time, not just another job. I still didn't have my high school diploma, but a lifelong friend made me a deal.

She said, "If you study for the GED and take the test, I'll pay the fee." I took her up on it, and that decision changed everything. It opened doors I didn't even know were possible for me.

I applied for a job with the State. It required a high school diploma or GED, and even though it was just a temp position, it came with benefits, something I had never had before.

A friend who worked there encouraged me to apply. I got the interview. I got the job. The schedule was good, lots of holidays and time off. The environment was stable. Safe. Predictable. After years of chaos, that alone felt like salvation.

The pay wasn't great, but the benefits were. And I knew one thing for sure: if I wanted to move up, I would need more education. Thanks to that friend who pushed me, now I could go to school.

By fall, I was registered for classes at the community college. I was so excited. I can't explain what it meant to me to be going to college, it felt like breathing after being underwater for years. After all the times I had been called a stupid, fat bitch, I wanted to stand on the highest rooftop and scream, "Who's stupid now?"

But I didn't. I just went to class, went to work, and tried to be a good mother to my two teenagers. Life moves fast. One day they were babies on my hip, now here we were.

That same year, Hurricane Katrina hit. Our office partnered with the car dealership I used to work at to help people displaced by the storm.

At a meeting at a local church, we helped them apply for state jobs, get fast-tracked interviews, and the dealership worked with those who had lost vehicles to get back on the road.

It felt good to do something meaningful in the middle of so much suffering.

It was there that I ran into an old coworker. He was actually on his way out when he looked back and saw me across the room.

Our eyes met. He gave me a little nod, just a simple Hey. I smiled, and he walked out. I went back to helping a young woman fill out her application when I suddenly felt two hands on my shoulders.

It was him.

He asked how I'd been. If I was working for the state. How the kids were. Just simple small talk, except he was flirting. And not just casual flirting.

That man could charm the paint off a wall. My heart was beating like a shy schoolgirl even though I knew he was married. But that didn't mean he wasn't cute. He always had been.

And the thing is, I didn't think anyone actually flirted with me. In my mind, I was still the stupid, fat, ugly bitch I had been told I was for so many years.

Those words don't just disappear because life gets better. They stay tucked in the corners of you, like cobwebs.

So, I just told myself he was being his usual playful self.

And maybe that would have been the end of it.

But it wasn't.

About a week passed after that community meeting at the church. I was sitting at my desk at work when the phone rang. I answered, and it was him.

He said he was just calling to check on the young woman I had been helping that night, wanted to know if she had gotten the job. He mentioned he was also trying to help her get a car, so it all sounded harmless enough at first.

But then the real reason for the call slipped out.

He said he wanted to see me.

And without even thinking, I said, "Hey, aren't you married?"

He paused for just a second and said, *"Yes... technically."*

Technically.
A word I will never forget for the rest of my life.

He went on to say that they were separated, that they were "about to file for divorce." And I'm not saying he was lying, maybe in that exact moment, maybe in his mind, that was the story he was telling himself and everyone else. But looking back, with older eyes and a clearer mind, I don't believe he ever had any real intention of divorcing her.

Because she was his meal ticket.

And I didn't know it at the time, but I was about to learn a very old lesson the very hard way:

Just because someone is unhappy doesn't mean they're leaving.

I agreed to meet him.

He drove over to my apartment that evening. I didn't let him come upstairs, my kids were home, and I wasn't about to have anybody around them like that. So, we sat outside and talked for a while. Then he said, "Let's take a drive."

I told the kids I'd be right back. He made up some story about needing to run down the street to check on something and wanted me to ride with him.

It was a ploy.

He took me down a dark back road, parked the truck, got out, walked around to my side, opened my door, and with that same cocky charm I remembered, he kissed me like I had never been kissed before in my life.

Lord have mercy.

Jesus *himself* probably had to look away.

Because that man was fine. And the way he kissed? My knees didn't just get weak, they quit their job, packed up, and moved out. I fell for him right then and there. Instantly. For this fool.

And here's the thing:

What's that saying going around these days?
"Jesus won't send you somebody else's husband."
No, He sure won't.

But the devil will.
And he did.

I knew better.

But sometimes knowing better and doing better aren't the same thing. And when you've been starved for attention, for affection, for feeling seen, really seen, it doesn't take much to send you tumbling.

We started a *thing*.
I can't even call it a relationship. It wasn't that. Not really.

I allowed myself to believe his lies because I was in love with him. In love in a way I had never experienced before. I had never known attention like this. He called me multiple times a day.

He wanted to know how my day was going. How the kids were doing in school. How I was doing in my school. He asked about my life, really asked, and listened like it mattered.

How could a man like this have marital issues?

In my mind, *there had to be something wrong with his "soon to be" ex-wife.*

Because he seemed perfect.

Isn't it wild how blind we are in the beginning?
We don't see red flags, we see fireworks.
We don't see patterns, we see potential.

We see what we want to see.

After a while, I realized he wasn't going to leave her. I told him I could not keep seeing a married man. He would tell me how miserable he was.

He told me he loved me, that he didn't love her. And the one that really got me, "I just can't leave my children with her."

Oh, how I believed that for far longer than I should have.

I even tried to date other people. But any time I tried to move on, he would get upset, beg me to *"please just wait for him."* And for a long time, I did.

Eventually, I met someone online. He was from out of town. We talked on the phone for about three months before we ever met in person.

He was about six years older than me, his father a preacher and his mother a teacher. He had a great sense of humor, and I genuinely enjoyed talking to him. It felt *easy.* Light. Something I hadn't felt in a while.

One day he told me he would be coming through and asked if he could stop by and take me to dinner. I was excited. The good kind of excited, nervous fluttery, hopeful excited. He said he'd be there around 6:00 PM.

It was a weeknight, the kids were home, and I told them, "Mom's got a date." They were just as excited as I was. They'd heard our conversations for months, sometimes laughing at me, sometimes teasing, but I could tell they were glad their mom was smiling again.

6:00 came and went.

7:00, he texted, said he was running late. I told myself no big deal.

8:00, he finally pulled up.

And there I was, hair done, makeup on, looking cute, and this man stepped out of the car wearing sweatpants, tennis shoes, and he was drunk.

He came inside and sat on the sofa like it was nothing. I asked, *"Aren't we going to dinner?"*
He shrugged and said, *"Yeah, but what's open around here this late that isn't about to close?"*

He wasn't wrong, but he was wrong.

He apologized and said he was nervous about meeting me and had too much to drink. Then he tried to kiss me. Wrong move, mister.

I told him he needed to leave. Or better yet, go get a hotel room because he was too drunk to drive back to home, and he damn sure wasn't staying at my house.

He looked shocked, like *he* was the one being mistreated.

And in that moment, standing in my living room in my nice shoes with that man in sweatpants looking like disappointment in human form, I realized something:

I was tired.

Tired of waiting.
Tired of excuses.
Tired of crumbs and calling it love.

And the man I *really* needed to be telling goodbye wasn't sitting on my couch.

He was the one who only loved me "technically."

A couple of years went by.

The "affair," which I was finally calling it out loud, went on and off like a porch light with bad wiring. No consistency. He loved me one week, ignored me for three. That was my love life for years, a constant state of waiting for crumbs.

During that time, I left my comfortable state job and jumped into the oil and gas industry. The money was great, but the hours were long and I was away from home more than I liked.

Time had gone by so fast. The kids were fast approaching adult hood. With this, they spent very little time with their dad. They might go over on a holiday for a few hours. But that was about it. My son pretty much stopped seeing his nanny due to him standing up to her one day and going against something she said.

As he grew, he realized she was not what she portrayed herself to be. It took a long time for him to see that and when it hit him, it hurt him deeply. He grew up thinking she would love him through anything, but the truth was, anything as long as it was her way. His dad was the same.

My son was grown now, moving into his first place. I remember standing in that little run-down house thinking, how did we get here so fast?

He was so proud of it, smiling ear to ear, and honestly, I think the place might have been where the homeless held committee meetings before he decided to pay actual money to live there.

But with his girlfriend, his sister, and me, we scrubbed that place down, hung curtains, and made it a home. He was working for the State then, so he could afford to keep it going. He was independent. He was happy.

My daughter was a senior in high school. I was blessed with such good kids. I worked late, and she worked at the Mexican restaurant in town, so we would usually walk in the door around the same time at night. We had this sweet little rhythm to our life. A nice home. A good job. The ability to go places and do things we had never been able to before. These years were some of our happiest.

I had a close group of girlfriends. I was always doing something with them, or with my sister on the weekends. I laughed a lot. I had joy. I had a life.

The only downside was him.

Sound familiar?

The only bad part of my life was the man who was trying to

control me, and I can't even fully blame him, because I allowed it. I allowed the emotional tug-of-war, the half-love, the waiting, the hoping, the way my heart lived in the in-between.

Eventually, I got offered a lucrative job in the city. So off we went, me and my daughter. She drove back and forth during the week to finish school and stayed with my sister until graduation.

Then she moved in with me. We made a life in the big city, a world away from the small towns we'd always known. We lived by the Galleria Mall, and we made memories, just me and her.

She eventually got a job working in the mailroom at the same company I did.
We really were building something, just the two of us.

But that job was *work*.
Oil and gas doesn't play.

The company demanded total loyalty. Day, night, weekends, didn't matter. If my boss emailed or texted at 10 PM, he expected a response at 10:01. Think The Devil Wears Prada, but make the boss a man and remove the fashion. That was my life.

A stark difference from the State, where 5:01 PM meant the building was empty and your life was your own.

This was the private sector.
You didn't just work there.
You *belonged* to it.

After a few years in the private sector, I decided to go back to the state. The money had been good, but the constant pressure had worn me down.

I got a job in a town about thirty minutes north of Dallas, and my daughter and I moved to a smaller city nearby. We hadn't been there long when my niece, now grown and married, needed my help.

She was pregnant and not doing well. Her husband was stationed at a Marine base, and she had been placed on bed rest. She needed someone she trusted. She needed me.

At the same time, my daughter had decided to go to college. So, we got her moved to a town with a community college.

She found a house to rent with a female police officer, and we got her enrolled in classes. I wasn't worried about her, she had always been strong, independent, resourceful.

And sure enough, she blossomed in her new life. She made new friends, found her place in the world, and stepped fully into her own.

Watching her grow into a kind, confident, well-rounded young woman… I was so proud of her.

My son was doing well too. He had met someone new, and they had moved in together. He was working, maintaining his own home, learning how to build a life. Both of my children were steady, grounded, and doing okay.

So, with everyone settled and taken care of, I packed up and headed to my niece's house, ready to stay for at least six months.

I didn't know it then, but that move would shift everything, again.

This move was another fresh start. To break old bonds and

create new ones.

I used that time break the bond *he* had over me. And it worked. Did I miss him? Yes. But it was for the best. The affair had gone on for years. It had its claws in my heart, and I needed distance to finally pull them out.

And now, my heart belonged to the tiny baby growing in my niece's belly.

Talk about never knowing love like this before.

The months we spent together before the baby was born were sweet. She got healthier and eventually came off bed rest.

I got a job at the local hospital, and on my days off we would go to the mall, buying baby clothes, fixing up the nursery, getting ready for this new chapter of our lives.

When that baby girl was born, a soft, warm, perfect bundle of joy, I felt something settle in me. Something good. Something hopeful.

But it was bittersweet. I wished more than anything that her mother, my sister, could have been there. And my mother. It broke my heart that neither of them would ever get to hold her, or any of the great grand babies.

And this wasn't my sister's first grandchild; my other niece had a son already. A rooting'-tooting' little cowboy with beautiful curly red hair, just like my sister's when she was a little girl.

He had my daddy wrapped clean around his finger. And thank God for that. Daddy lived just down the road from them then.

That little boy gave my dad his life back in a way none of us could.

Babies. What an incredible chapter they create, even in the middle of grief. They weren't my grands, but they were my Greats!

Christmastime came and I flew back home to be with my kids. We went to my son's house and had our little Christmas together. My son told me that his dad had stopped by his house a few times to see him. At first, I thought that was great. But then he told me that his dad was stopping to borrow money from him. I was shocked.

He said he thought his dad had a drug problem and definitely a drinking problem. His dad had been living with a woman for years, but I guess they had split up. I didn't keep in touch with him in any way so I had no idea what kind of life he was living. Didn't care either. Other than that, we had a great time together and then I flew back to my niece's house to spend my time with a little baby girl.

I ended up staying about nine months with my niece before we all moved back to home together. Those months will always be sacred to me.

My two nieces, girls who grew up without a mother, who were abused by their fathers, were now mothers themselves.

Strong, gentle, loving women. I was proud of them in a way I can't explain. Proud of what they survived. Proud of what they built.

The beauty that can rise out of tragedy is something to behold.

Back at home, I took a job at a small, family-owned business as the office manager. I was doing well. I had even bought an RV and moved it out to a little park in the country. I didn't know my next move yet, but the RV felt right, simple, mine, easy to pick up and go if needed.

It was just me now. No kids to take care of. Just peace.

And Carly Jo.

A tiny Yorkie with a big personality, my little ride-or-die. She went everywhere with me. That dog held a piece of my heart in her tiny paws.

Life was simple then.
Not perfect. But peaceful. And peace felt like a miracle.

Then I ran into him.

CHAPTER EIGHT: THE WRONG KINDS OF LOVE

Remember the song by Dolly Parton, Here You Come Again? That's how I felt when I saw him, the man I'd had an affair with.

He was working at a small dealership in the same town where I had my RV parked. God, he was hard to resist. I stopped one day and said hello.

He gave me a hug, asked how I'd been doing, and we caught up. He asked for my number. I gave it to him, knowing it was the wrong thing to do.

It only took him two hours before he was texting me. Wanting to know where I was staying. If I was seeing anyone. Of course, he asked about the kids too, but that was just the warm-up. Casual small talk to slide into the real conversation he wanted to have.

We texted back and forth for a few days, and then he asked if he could stop by on his way home one night. I said sure.

He stepped inside. No words. Just that familiar pull between us. The kind that didn't need explaining. We fell into each other the way we always had, like muscle memory, like something both of us knew by heart.

There was a part of me that truly believed he loved something about me. The same way I loved something about him.

But we both knew it would never work. And that was the last time I ever saw him romantically again.

The distance from him for so long had done its job. Yes, I saw him again, but the grip he once had on me had finally loosened.

His charm did not land the way it used to. The spell was gone. Maybe I was stronger now. Maybe I had simply grown up. Or maybe, after all those years stumbling through the dark, I had finally learned how to see the forest for the trees.

And for the first time in my life, I didn't chase the kind of love that hurt me to have.

Months went by and I enjoyed being single and free. I spent time with the babies in the family, with my kids, my dad, my sister, my friends.

I filled my days doing things I liked again. I had moved to a new RV park where I had a little more privacy, even a small yard.

In the evenings, Carly Jo and I would sit outside and watch the sun go down. Sometimes I'd start a small fire, and a friend would come over. We'd drink a beer and laugh. It was simple. It was peaceful. It was mine.

But late at night, I'd get on Facebook and scroll through everyone posting their happy relationships and perfect lives.

And I guess I got lonely.

I started feeling like maybe there was *more* out there than what I was living. So, I started searching again. For what, I didn't know. I just knew I felt something missing.

I got on a dating website again, and that's where I met my future husband.

We weren't strangers. We had a few mutual acquaintances. I'd seen him in passing before, but we'd never spoken. We started messaging one night, and after a few evenings of texting, he asked me to dinner.

He wasn't my usual type. He didn't flirt. He didn't have lines. He wasn't trying to impress me or seduce me. He was easy to be around, the kind of fun you have when you're sitting around with your closest friends, laughing about nothing and everything.

We discovered we both loved garage sales. So, for our next date, we got up early on a Saturday and hit yard sales together. Then lunch. Just talking. Laughing. Finding little treasures for a dollar. It was one of the best dates I had ever been on.

I actually looked forward to seeing him again.

We did this for a couple of months. Then one day, he asked me to move in. Not in a romantic way, just practical. He knew I lived in an RV and was thinking about selling it. He told me he had an extra bedroom and could use help with rent.

So, I moved in. I had started a new job that was about an hour away, working 12-hour shifts, 9 a.m. to 9 p.m. By the time

I got home, it was close to 10. He would have dinner waiting. He played with Carly Jo, kept her company. We'd watch junk TV, I'd shower, and go to bed, in my own room. Weekends were garage sales, movies, just being together. We had a sweet, easy life. Best friends, really.

Then one night, we kissed. And we let it go further. That's how we became a couple.

We moved into a two-story house that was way too big for us. My son and his girlfriend rented the upstairs. We stayed downstairs. It felt like one big, busy, happy home. We were good.

And eventually, marriage felt like the next step. Before I even realized what was happening, I was planning a wedding and changing my last name again.

My daughter was still living her best life, she had actually moved to a small town with her best friend. She was doing very well there, had gotten involved in Church and was the nursery caretaker for most Sunday and Wednesday evening services. She stayed in touch with her dad from time to time.

He had met a woman and they had a child together. She went to the hospital to see the baby when it was born. My daughter had a great little life for herself and I was a proud Moma.

Three days before the wedding, I came home exhausted and went to bed early. He woke me up and told me I needed to call my daughter. There had been an explosion in her town. I knew she would've been at church.

I called. No answer.
Called again. No answer.

Panic.

Half-dressed, shoes barely on, I grabbed my purse and we drove, fast.

When we got there, the whole town was chaos. Sirens. Smoke. The sky on fire. Streets blocked. I couldn't get to her. I thought I was going to lose my mind.

She had been at church working in the nursery when the fertilizer plant exploded. The church had taken a hit, but they were okay. Her house, though, was gone. A huge piece of debris had landed right in the middle of it and burned everything she owned to the ground. She was devastated.

She came home with us.

And that's when the truth hit me, I didn't want to go through with the wedding.

I couldn't say it out loud then. But I knew.

I loved him. I did. But I was not *in* love with him. We were best friends. We had sex, yes. But there was no *lovemaking.* No ache. No urgency. No fire.

I kept convincing myself that the "in love" part would come later. That surely love would grow. That fun and stability and kindness were enough.

So, I walked down the aisle anyway. I stood in front of God and everyone I loved, and promised forever.

Why didn't anyone stop me?
Why didn't I stop myself?

One person did try. My lifelong best friend told me it wouldn't last. I got mad at her for saying it, but deep down, I already knew she was right.

Because we were friends.
Not lovers.
And I married him anyway.

A few months after we were married, we decided to move to the city. More to do, better job opportunities, nothing holding us back. We had a huge garage sale, got rid of a bunch of stuff, and headed back to the big city.

I was nervous though. The kids' dad had just up and moved out of state, back to his hometown. No goodbye. No explanation. Just gone. Same way his mother had done about a year before.

One day there, the next day gone. I still don't even know how everyone found out, I think maybe someone he was living with called my daughter. It doesn't really matter. What mattered was how it felt.

It hurt both of my kids deeply that he didn't say goodbye. Didn't try. Didn't *care* enough to show up for them. And while I couldn't fix that, I wasn't about to create another wound on top of it.

So, before we moved, I sat them down. I asked them how they felt. If they were okay. If they were comfortable. Me living in the city wasn't new to them, we'd lived there before, but I wanted them to feel secure.

To know I wasn't going anywhere. That I wouldn't disappear. That I wasn't leaving them.

They said they were fine with it.

But I still carried the worry with me.

Sometimes, the hardest part of being a mother is loving your children through someone else's absence.

I went back to work for the state, and he'd got a job at a local hospital in the records department. We both made decent money, and life was… fine. Weekends were thrift store runs, movies, and taking the dogs to the park. Easy. Routine. Comfortable.

Then the depression hit. It knocked me out flat. I couldn't get out of bed. I hated my job. I hated the city. And deep down, I knew I had made a mistake. He didn't understand. He thought we were happy. And I couldn't bring myself to say it out loud.

Eventually, I pulled myself back together and got another job at a big hospital. I made friends there, real friends. Women who carried me through the next three years.

Don't get me wrong, I wasn't miserable every day. We had good times. But I always knew the ending was coming. Because that deep, real, in-your-bones kind of love wasn't there.

He picked up a side job delivering groceries for extra money. He was always good at hustling a little extra so we could have fun. But I noticed the money wasn't showing up in the bank account. I noticed him taking his phone with him every time he took the trash out. The laptop always shut and locked. Small things, but women know. We always know.

One evening, I told him to go grab BBQ from our favorite

spot. He left, and for the first time, he hadn't closed his laptop. I sat down, opened it, and there it was. Emails. Messages. Another woman.

I wasn't angry. A little hurt, yes. But mostly, relieved. This was my out.

When he came home and I confronted him, he threw a fit like I'd never seen. He shouted that *I* had betrayed *his* trust. The irony was almost laughable.

I didn't respond. I didn't yell. I let him have his tantrum. He left that night and stayed in a hotel. Eventually, he came back and we talked.

The truth was, we both felt the same. The "in-love" was missing. The butterflies. The spark. The pull. We cared about each other, but we were not each other's forever.

I suggested we stay roommates until we could move out separately. And that's what we did.

By the end of November, we had two different apartments. He kept the car because I lived two blocks from work. I walked or took the bus and saved for another car. He still picked me up to take me to the grocery store sometimes. We were ending the marriage the same way we began it: as friends. And that mattered to me.

A few months passed. I got a new car and a new apartment. It was February when an old friend messaged me on social media and asked if I had gotten divorced, said he noticed I changed my last name back.

I told him I was separated and we'd be filing soon.

He said he was separated too. I felt sad for him because I thought they were happy. But that's what everyone thought about me too.

We talked for hours. Laughed about junior high. He told me he had a crush on me back then. He said to holler at him next time I was in town; he'd cook fish. He loved to fish.

Turns out, I was going to be in town that weekend for Valentine's Day. He said, perfect. Come Saturday. Dinner.

And that was the beginning of a love story that nearly destroyed me.

Even now, years later, it hurts to write this. Because I still care for him. I've known him since kindergarten. And yet I want nothing to do with him ever again.

His lies and his darkness tore me apart. It was more than cheating. More than yelling or cussing or fighting. He broke me down piece by piece. He wanted to ruin me as a woman. As a person. As a human being.

No one had ever spoken to me the way he spoke to me. Not even my first husband.

And with all the ways to communicate now, text, social media, email, messenger, he had endless ways to hurt me. Endless ways to apologize. Endless ways to reel me back in. He was both the angel and the devil.

And he had a meth pipe in his pocket the whole time.

He called my mother a whore, a woman he never met. My

mother who was with one man her whole life. He called my children names.

He told me my body looked like an alien. Then he would fall to pieces, crying, saying he should kill himself for saying those things.

He was sick. Deeply. Mentally ill and addicted to meth. And from the very first night, everything between us was built on lies.

He told me he and his wife had simply fallen out of love, that the divorce was peaceful and mutual. In reality, he was still sleeping with her, along with several other women at the same time.

I would let him in, then throw him out, over and over, like I was trying to save myself and save him at the same time.

I tried to move on. I even dated a good man for a short time, one of the best I've ever known. He was handsome, steady, respected. He treated me with patience and tenderness, never asking for anything I couldn't give.

He knew the damage that had been done to me and never held it against me. And still, I pushed him away.

Explain to me why my heart ran toward the fire instead of the hands trying to carry me out.

The man I kept going back to couldn't hold a job. He used openly. He took and took and gave nothing back. I convinced myself that if I could just get his life steady, if I could just hold him together long enough, maybe he would become the man I thought I saw in him once.

Then he got arrested, again. I think it was the third time in a year. Prison was unavoidable this time. He begged me to stand by him. Told me that sobriety would change everything, that once he got clean, he would love me the way he should have all along.

And I believed him.

So, I waited.

Every Saturday for six months, I drove three hours one way to see him for one hour. Then drove three hours back home. I worked two jobs to make sure he had food money and phone money.

And how long did it take him to use meth after he got out?

Two weeks.

He left and went to his mother's.

One day, I will write the whole story. But not yet. It still burns.

So, I bought another RV. Bought a little piece of land. And me and Carly Jo went back to the country.

Just me and my dog.
Starting over.
Yet, again.

CHAPTER NINE: STARTING OVER, YET AGAIN

Three acres. Doesn't seem like much to some people, but to me it was heaven. I had a view to the east and west, so I got both the sunrise and the sunset. But the nights were the best.

OH MY GOSH, the stars. Me and Carly Jo would sit outside after dark, never afraid, just peaceful.

For the first time, I was in love with something that couldn't leave me. Not a man. Not a house. Not a dream of what could be. I was in love with a feeling.

A feeling of belonging, of being exactly where I was supposed to be.

I had some close friends a few miles down the road. When I first moved onto the land, they came over and helped me mow, trim, haul, whatever needed doing. I appreciated it, but I also did a lot myself. I *liked* doing it.

Every day after work, I was doing something outside. And at the end of each day, I would grab an old bucket, and me and Carly Jo would walk the property and pick up rocks.

Sometimes my son would come help. We'd walk slow, talk, laugh, and cover every inch of the place like it was treasure. And in a way, it was.

I made flowerbeds out of those rocks. One rock at a time.

My son had been going through his own hard things. After I got married, he developed a seizure disorder. The doctors never could figure out why. It took a toll on him and the relationship he'd been in for years.

They eventually broke up. He later married a girl he'd dated in high school. She had a little boy who was four, and my son loved that child instantly. They got married, but it didn't last either. They weren't meant to be husband and wife. But that little boy stayed his heart. So, he stayed "Dad."

Now my son was living in an apartment in town. He came out to see me three or four times a week. My place was peaceful. He liked it there. He'd bring his guitar, and we'd build a fire, drink a couple beers, and play music. Sometimes he'd bring his boy, who by now was calling him Dad. He was six then.

My nephew and his wife would come too, and their little boy would play and run wild with him. Those were some of the happiest evenings I have ever had.

I was back working for the state as an inspector. I loved my job. My son was still working for the state too. I was slowly getting my land the way I wanted it.

I bought a small cabin shell and worked on finishing it out, bit by bit. I got the electricity done. Then started on the water lines. I was still living in my camper, but I bought a big metal carport to put over it so it would stay cool and protected.

I can't explain the happiness of that time. I had never made a wiser decision than buying that land. It filled an empty space in me I didn't even know had been hollow all along.

But my son's seizures were getting worse. He couldn't keep himself organized, didn't keep his meds filled on time, didn't always eat right, didn't have the structure he needed to stay stable.

So, I told him to move into the cabin and I would stay in the RV. I could always buy a mobile home and put it on the back of the property later. So that's what we did.

I helped him keep his meds straight, made sure he didn't miss doses, and I cooked for us so he stayed steady. When you have seizures like his, routine is everything. He had been having them for years, grand mal seizures, the kind that leave you exhausted and confused for days.

His brain had been through so much trauma. I could see the forgetfulness growing, the confusion, the frustration. I was glad he was close to me again. And it meant something to have someone beside me to watch the stars at night.

He loved it like me and Carly Jo did.

During the summer months at the cabin, my niece would bring her girls over. She had three girls now. They call me Mammie.

They loved to come to Mammie's house and we would swim in my small above ground pool. We had such good times. They'd help me plant flowers and play with the dogs. At night, they would roast marshmallows by the fire and make s'mores.

Good times and beautiful memories.

One funny memory I would love to share with you:

One day I was working on a table my best friend and I had bought at a garage sale. I had it flipped upside down, working on the legs, and when I went to step over it, I fell.

The pain was instant and extremely sharp, I knew I had broken my leg. I sat up and started looking for my phone. Of course, it was on the other side of the room.

So, I dragged myself to it and called my friend.

Now, let me explain something about my friend: she never answers her phone.
Ever.
You will die in a ditch before that girl answers a phone call.

But like an idiot, I called her first.

No answer.

Called again.

Still no answer.

So, I texted her:

"Answer the damn phone; I broke my damn leg."

A few minutes later she replied:

"You're lying." I laughed out loud.

Eventually, she showed up and took me to the hospital.

My days were filled with work and evenings filled with sitting on my swing watching the sun go down.

My friend would come over on weekends and we would drink coffee and talk.

Sometimes she'd come at night and we'd build a fire and have a drink and talk all night long.

Then Covid hit. Everything came to a stop. What a weird period of time. I couldn't do my normal inspections. My job was all about traveling. I covered 19 counties doing inspections at different jobsites. Not anymore. Not until they figured this out.

I ended up working from home for Department of State Health Services, doing interviews over the phone for people who had contracted Covid and taking information and doing interviews for all the people who may have been exposed.

I received two special state awards for doing that work. It was long, mentally draining work, 12 hours a day on the phone and computer.

My son was at home from work due to his seizures, so times were tough and strange.

He was also going through personal issues with his ex-wife. She was attempting to reconnect her son with his biological father.

His real dad had never been a part of his life. And now suddenly she wanted to introduce them. This was tearing my son apart.

Not because he didn't want him to know his real dad, but because he could feel what was coming next.

He was at a low point in life. His marriage didn't work out, his girlfriend didn't work out, his job was on the fritz, his seizures were destroying his brain, and now he might be losing the only thing that he really loved, who loved him too, the only son he would ever have.

One night, I was sitting out by the fire. My son had been out to his ex-wife's house to see his son. He received some devastating news.

They were going to stop allowing him to come visit. They wanted to eventually terminate the relationship between my son and his son.

I am assuming so that he could get to know his real father. My son was beyond devastated. He was inconsolable.

We sat and talked for a while. I tried to tell him that he would be okay and that plans don't always work like people want them to.

That even if they wanted to do this, his son would find his way back to him.

Nothing made him feel better. And I can't imagine how he felt. I had never been in the position he was in.

He said he wanted to be alone, and I understood. I told him that I had to go into the office the next morning, but that I would check on him before I left.

I watched him slowly walk to the cabin. The glow of the fire on his back.

The next morning, I got up and got ready for work. I made my coffee and realized I didn't have any sweetener for my coffee.

I knew there was some in the cabin, so I decided to sneak in quietly and see if he was awake and grab some.

I opened the door. The cabin is an open concept, so you can see the entire room except the bathroom.

The lights were on.

The bed was made, or maybe hadn't been slept in.

His shoes were beside the bed, his cigarettes on the bedside table.

I called his name, but he didn't answer.

I walked over to the counter to get the Sweet 'N Low, thinking maybe he was outside and I just didn't see him. So, I walked outside and called his name again.

No answer.

Then it dawned on me. He's had a seizure!

I ran back inside the cabin and went straight to the bathroom.

There he was on the floor. He was blue.

I screamed.

It took me a moment to understand what I was looking at. He didn't have a seizure.

He had hung himself.

But he had fallen. He was slumped between the wall and the toilet. He had used a bar at the top of the ceiling and an extension cord, the green one I had used for Christmas lights the year before.

I guess during the night, the cord stretched and slowly lowered him to the floor.

I called 911 in a panic and told them what happened. They asked about CPR, but I told them he was cold and blue and had no pulse.

I just cried and said, "You didn't say goodbye."

Within moments, my house was flooded with first responders who lived just down the road, then the sheriff's department, ambulance, and fire department.

I walked out of the cabin and onto the porch where he and I had sat together so many days.

And in the midst of all the chaos and noise, I heard nothing. I felt nothing. I was numb.

Until a breeze blew up behind me, and I heard a voice say, "Mom, I'm okay."

As if his soul moved through me to let me know not to worry.

And in that moment, I swear I could remember exactly what his tiny head smelled like the day he was born.

That warm, sweet, innocent smell. I think it's the smell of our soul. Because only newborn babies have that scent.

That day was a complete blur. All I remember is crying, shock, and the look on my daughter's face when I saw her for the first time.

I've always heard people say that losing a child leaves a hole in your gut that you can't describe. And that's the truth. I feel like a piece of my body is missing.

I guess since he came from my body, that's how my mind makes sense of losing him. But it literally feels like there is a hole in my stomach. And nothing can fill it.

My son always said he wanted to be cremated, so that's what we did. We had a small, simple service in the church where he attended and served as a child.

His dad did not come. But they sent a plant. Never heard another word from him.

After a few days, I went back to my land. I couldn't go into the cabin. I crawled up into my RV and slept for days. It was wintertime.

The perfect season to shut yourself away and hide from the world.

Thank God I had a wonderful team of people I worked with who donated enough sick time for me to take off work for the next few months and still get paid. And that is exactly what I did.

I slept when I wanted to.
Cried when I wanted to.
Threw a tantrum when I needed to.
I broke things.
I burned things.

All of it was therapeutic.

Someone made me a plate of weed cookies. I am not a weed smoker, but I ate them all. Every last single one. Every crumb.

My son would have thought that was hilarious. And I giggled at that thought.

After about a month, I made the decision to go inside the cabin. I don't know why, but I had to leave the front door open. I know that sounds strange, but for some reason when I went inside, I started to feel claustrophobic.

I mean, I know now that it was anxiety, trauma, panic, all of it. But leaving the front door open helped me breathe. So, I did. One day at a time, one foot in front of the other, until I could start going through some things.

Then the anger set in.

And I began to burn furniture.

I dragged the sofa out. The bed. Anything that felt heavy or haunted or painful. I built a big bonfire and lit it like a mad woman. But it was therapeutic. It was necessary. It was me screaming without making a sound.

After the bonfire and the cleaning, I started finishing the things we hadn't done yet to the cabin.

I told myself; *I can do this. I can fix it and live in it.* And I tried. I really did. I fixed it up so cute. It was everything I wanted it to be.

But I couldn't shake the claustrophobic feeling.

I kept having flashes of his face. His cold, blue face. It would come out of nowhere. Just hit me. Like a punch to the chest.

It wasn't him haunting me, it was the trauma. It was the moment. The last image. The kind of memory that stamps itself onto your mind and won't let go.

I tried to stay there. I really did.

But I couldn't.

I made the decision to sell the land and the cabin. I had to say goodbye to everything. To my son, and to the memories.

It was the hardest decision I've ever made, but I knew I couldn't stay in that space anymore. I couldn't keep reliving that morning.

I had one last bonfire.
Just me, the fire, and the sky.

I took some of his ashes and threw them into the flames, and I watched them rise up with the heat, lifting, dancing, disappearing into the night air.

It was beautiful.
It was heartbreaking.
It was release.

I left that place with no real clue or plan, just wandering. I was in a fog, moving on instinct. In the summer, I made the decision to leave my job with the state. It was wild and sporadic, but I did it.

I took the retirement money out of my account. And from

there, it was one crazy ride after another.

I took off to South Carolina for a month with a girl who needed help moving. Then I came back home and stayed with my niece for a while, until we got into a huge fight.

After that, I ended up at my daughter's house, and that's where everything caught up with me.

All the trauma.
All the grief.
All the PTSD.

It hit me like a vengeance.

In the span of four months, I had three different jobs. All of which I quit, mainly because I was not mentally stable at the time. I eventually sought counseling and medication and finally started piecing my life back together.

It's funny looking back now, but picture this:

I thought working at a daycare around babies would make me feel better.

So, there I was, sitting in a room full of crying babies.
Not happy babies.
Not giggling, cooing babies.
Crying babies. All of them.

I stood up, walked straight to the office, and said, "You need to come replace me right now. I got to go."

I grabbed my purse, drove to Starbucks, ordered two cream cheese Danishes, and sat in the parking lot crying and eating both of them like my life depended on it.

It wasn't funny at the time.
But me and my daughter laugh hysterically at it now.

My son, would also get a kick out of this.

Recovery is a long, twisted road, full of potholes, detours, and stretches where you can't see two feet in front of you. You just keep going anyway.

CHAPTER TEN: THIS IS NOT MY LAST CHAPTER

Making the decision to move back to the area where I was raised, and where I raised my children, was mostly about comfort. I needed to be somewhere familiar, somewhere that felt like it still knew me.

It was hard at first, because everything reminded me of my son. But as time went on, I realized that was actually the part I liked the most.

There are moments when I regret selling my land and think maybe I should have only sold the cabin. But regret does no good for the soul.

I allow those thoughts to come in, I sit with them for a moment, and then I release them, like dust dancing in a beam of light.

I applied for a position at a facility where I first began my career with the state. I interviewed with a woman I could tell right away had immense integrity. You can see that in a person's eyes. And she had it, a lot of it.

It was hard in the beginning, because this is where my son worked when he died. Many of his coworkers are still here, still in that same department.

But now, like before, it brings me comfort.

A few months after coming back, I was walking across the parking lot near the building where he worked.

I noticed a shiny purple pen on the ground.

I picked it up immediately because purple is my son's birthstone. Then I read the engraving, and I almost lost my breath.

It said:

"Life may not be the party we hoped for, but while we're here, we should dance."

Those were the exact words his sister spoke at his funeral.

Don't tell me the dead aren't still with us.
Because that was my son, 100%.

That was his way of saying,
"Hey Mom. Love you."

I still have that pen propped up by his picture, that last picture that he and I ever took together, one month before he died.

My family has history at this facility where I work. My mom and dad both worked here when I was a child.

I work here now, and my son worked here too. Three

generations of us have walked these grounds.

My mom went to nursing school and became a nurse here. My dad worked in the maintenance department, the same one that sits right across from where I live now.

I live in employee housing, on campus, in the very house my dad helped work on and take care of.

Recently, they replaced all the windows in this old house. I asked if I could keep them. They were the original 9-pane windows from back in the 60s. My dad came and picked them up and built me a beautiful greenhouse out of them, so I could put my plants inside.

I will treasure it forever.

Securing a position out here brought back a familiar feeling of stability and security, something I lost after my son died.

Tragedy like that can make you lose yourself. It can scatter you in a thousand directions you don't recognize.

So, finding a place that makes you feel grounded again, it's valuable.
It's necessary.
It's life-saving.

From the moment I walked through those old familiar doors, I knew I had made the right decision. Even though there were days when doubt crept in, I allowed myself to feel it.

I let the thoughts come so I could sort through them, understand them, and figure out what they were trying to tell me.

Learning to let your thoughts come, to hold them, and to stay still long enough for life to reveal what you need to know, that is a rare and valuable thing. One that has taken me a very long time to master. But it has paid off.

At night, when I look out my bedroom window, I can see the soft glow of the lights over at the maintenance department.

It reminds me of when we used to bring Daddy to work early in the mornings. I can still remember riding up that same road and seeing those same lights.

I made the decision to move on campus because it is affordable, secure, and familiar. I feel safe here.
Safe in a way I hadn't felt in a long time.

During my second year here, my daughter and her husband were having some issues. She needed to fall apart, and he didn't know how to let her.

She had been so strong for me after her brother's death that, truthfully, it was her turn.

So, she came to stay with me.

We thought it would be permanent.
She moved down, brought all her things.

And then she slept.

And I let her.

That's what she needed. She had carried too much for too long. I wanted her to relax. Not worry about buying groceries.

Not worry about washing clothes, paying bills, keeping it

together. I just wanted her to fall apart and rest. To let go. To finally exhale.

She deserved that.

After a month, she slowly started picking herself back up. She started applying for jobs and eventually landed a position here on campus in the psychiatric, department.

I can't say she loved her job, because she didn't, but she was beginning to feel like herself again.

We began to enjoy each other's company and we fell into an old familiar routine. Like Home.

Home isn't where everything was perfect.
Home is where I remembered who I was.

After about six months, she remembered who she was and she returned to her husband.

I think God led me here. To this place, to this exact moment in my life, so that I would have a safe and stable home for her to come and fall apart in, safely, warmly, and comfortably. A place where she didn't have to be strong anymore.

Or maybe it was her brother who led us here.
Maybe he knew we would both need somewhere soft to land.

Working back here made me think a lot about my mother. How she went to school to better herself, to build a career that would support her family and leave a legacy.

That pushed me to finish my bachelor's degree. I know without a doubt that both my mom and my son would have been so proud of me.

Since moving back, I've been working hard on a lot of things. One of the most important has been making memories with my great-nieces and nephew.

That summer, I took my four little great-nieces, and my daughter, to the beach for a few days. After being cramped in a tiny condo and surviving Rainforest Café with all of them, my daughter informed me on the drive home that she is 1,000% sure she does not want children. So, these great-nieces are probably the only grandchildren I'll ever have.

And that's okay.
Because I am already their grandmother in all the ways that matter.

It has been important to me that they come to my home, see how I live, do fun things, and make memories. When I was little, I had a great-aunt who I was close to. My Auntie.

I have vivid memories of making things with her, noticing the plants in her garden, and spending the night at her house. She was the kindest person I ever knew.

I want my greats to have those memories, too.

I've been making more dates with my sister. We try to meet up at least once a month and have dinner somewhere.

We go to garage sales and community trade days together. She's got lots of grands, so anytime I need a baby fix, she's, my dealer!

Recently me and my sister went on a trip with my dad to see his sister. They are both getting older and he wanted to go and see her, so off we went.

Dad fell outside a while back and ended up laying outside in the heat for 8 hours. Had to spend the night in the hospital. So, I'm also making more of an effort to go see him each week.

He doesn't drive anymore, so the last time he did drive to see me is to pick up those windows. Now I will have that memory forever.

I'm making the effort to create memories. Because in the end, that's all we truly have to hold on to.

I was wandering through a thrift store one afternoon when I saw a familiar face. It was that sweet boy who used to be my son's shadow, the two of them were inseparable.

It took me a minute to realize who he was. My ex-husband's stepbrother. The stepson of my former mother-in-law.

He came up and hugged me so tight. Asked how my daughter was doing. Told me about his kids and how life had been treating him. And let me tell you, how that boy grew up to be so kind-hearted, I'll never know.

My ex-mother-in-law was awful to him. Controlling. Cold. She treated him like he was a burden, not a child.

He told me that my ex-husband was very sick, dying of throat cancer, but that he was given strict instructions by his mom not to tell me or my daughter.

I asked him why, and he just shrugged, like, *yeah… we both know she's crazy.* And we do.

I didn't say anything about it. I just bragged on his kids and wished him well. I told him to keep me posted and that it would stay between us.

I made a decision that day. I already knew I wanted to go on and get my master's, but I just hadn't been sure in what.

Standing there, talking to him, thinking about everything and everyone we had all survived, and everything we didn't... it hit me.

I chose clinical mental health counseling.

Because there are too many people walking around with wounds no one can see. Too many people carrying pain they don't have words for.

And too many people who needed help long before anyone realized something was wrong.

I wanted to be someone who could sit in that space with them. Someone who could actually do something.

Not just watch the damage happen and call it life.

Leave a legacy for my daughter.

A few months later, I did a Google search on my ex-husband. I don't even know what made me look, just a feeling.

I learned that he had passed away on May 1st. I called my daughter and told her. She was upset that nobody from his family had bothered to let her know.

I found out near the end of May. And then, on Father's Day weekend, her Nanny sent her a Facebook message telling her that her dad had died, and she thought she would "want to know."

MY LAST LETTER TO ALABAMA

Father's Day.

That's when she chose to tell her.

How cold-hearted do you have to be to send your granddaughter a message like that on Father's Day? About her father who died over a month ago? Like it was just some piece of gossip she forgot to mention earlier.

It felt cruel. Deliberate. The kind of cruelty that isn't loud, but sharp.

The kind that leaves a scar.

That day I wrote a letter.
My last letter to Alabama.

I had so much to say to that woman, and it had to come out. I had held my tongue for far too long.

All the years of swallowing my hurt, all the times I tried to keep the peace, all the moments I stayed quiet just to keep from causing waves, it all rose up at once.

I sat down and I wrote it.
Not to change anything.
Not to get an apology. But because I needed to say it.

For me. And I think to myself:

I still remember what I told him back when our babies were small, after he took that mesquite switch to me. I told him that one day he'd think of all this, what he did to us, behind a pack of cigarettes and a can of Skoal.

And sometimes I wonder, in those final breaths, lying there dying from throat cancer, if the memory finally came for him.

I pray it did.

That was the day I stopped carrying what wasn't mine anymore.

CHAPTER ELEVEN: FEELS LIKE HOME

I look at my life now and I know the truth.
My life is full. I can sit on my porch with my daughter, my sister, my nieces, and feel joy rise in my chest for no reason at all.

The kind of joy that does not need a reason or a story behind it. Just breath. Just peace.

I watch the hummingbirds fly in close to the feeders I hung. I pet my cat when it rubs against my leg. I feel the breeze move across my skin and I listen to the leaves rustling in the wind.

And I realize there is nowhere else I would rather be. There is nothing missing here. Nothing undone. Nothing broken.

Sometimes, in that stillness, I feel my son there too. Not in words. Not in signs I have to decipher.

Just in the breeze that comes up behind me the same way it did on the porch, the day he left this world.

It catches me off guard the same way.

Holds me still the same way.

And for a moment, I know he is with us.

Part of the peace I live in now. Part of the quiet

This is the life I dreamed of when I could not see how I would ever get here.

This is the life I fought for. This is the life I earned.

No amount of money could ever replace the worth of these simple, sacred days. These mornings. These children.These women who sit beside me and know they are loved. I know my strength will live on in them.

In the little ones who will grow up knowing that even when life tries to break us, we rise.

We are a strong group of women.
Not because life was gentle.
But because we did not surrender.

This is healing.
This is peace.
This is my life.
And I am finally home.

MY LAST LETTER TO ALABAMA

I think about her sometimes, that little girl I used to be.

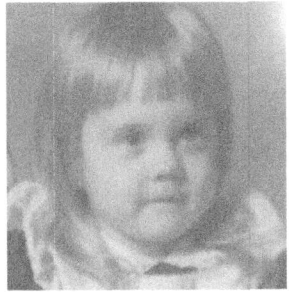

The one who kept getting up when she had every reason to stay down.

I didn't know it then, but I was building myself, piece by piece, out of every hard day I thought would break me.

When I look back now, I feel a mix of pride, protection, and a kind of gentle heartbreak, because I know what it cost her to survive.

There's one moment I carry softly, the day my daddy came to my apartment and put those chairs together. I remember standing there with that quiet pull in my gut. Not fear. Not panic. Just knowing. Something in me said, *pay attention*. And I didn't. I talked myself out of it. I told myself I was imagining things. I wanted to believe everything was okay. I wanted to believe I was safe.

If I could go back to her, I would push the words out of her mouth. I would scream to her, LEAVE!

I would take her face in my hands and say:

You are right.
You feel it.
You know.

You aren't crazy.

You aren't dramatic.

You are right.
Trust your gut instinct and leave.

I spent years learning how to hear myself again. To separate my true voice from fear.

To tell the difference between old wounds and present warnings. To walk through this world without abandoning myself.

Healing wasn't a grand moment or a single day. It was learning to trust the sound of my own soul again.

If you are reading this and something inside you is whispering, listen.

You do not need proof.
You do not need permission.
You do not need the world to agree with what you feel.

Your gut is not loud, but it is loyal. It tries to save you long before life collapses.

We do not get to choose what was done to us. But we do get to choose what we carry forward.

I chose to carry truth.
I chose to carry peace.
I chose to come home to myself.

And if you are in the middle of your own storm, hear me:

You are not too late to choose yourself, too.

Made in the USA
Coppell, TX
08 March 2026

73213870R00083